A Flask of Fields

Verbal and Visual Gems from the Films of W.C. Fields

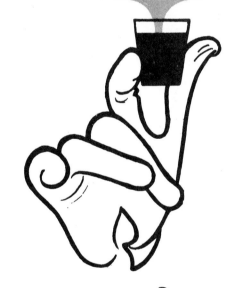

Edited by
Richard J. Anobile

Introduction by Judith Crist

Darien House Inc.

Pictures and dialogues from the following films are
used with the permission of Universal City Studios, Inc.

Tillie and Gus
International House
You're Telling Me
It's a Gift
Man on the Flying Trapeze
The Old Fashioned Way
My Little Chickadee
You Can't Cheat an Honest Man
Never Give a Sucker an Even Break
The Bank Dick

Library of Congress Catalogue Card Number: 72-88687

A Darien House book,
distributed by Bonanza Books,
a division of Crown Publishers

Designed by Harry Chester and Alexander Soma

Printed in the United States of America.

For Ulla

Contents

FOREWORD

The fact that we enjoy Fields today is ample indication of the mastery of the man. The fact that we can't always see his films, but, nonetheless, enjoy recalling scenes and sequences is my justification for this book.

There are over 700 frame blow-ups here. No stills, no publicity shots. Every photo used to illustrate scenes from the films can be found on screen, and the dialogue has been transcribed directly from the films. I had first proposed the idea of using frame blow-ups for a book that was released last year titled WHY A DUCK? It was a compilation of scenes from the films of the Marx Bros. The publisher was justifiably worried about the cost of the book, which zoomed above that of ordinary film books. Even Groucho, who wrote the introduction, was openly skeptical of the project. But eventually the book came out; the first printing was sold out before the official publication date. Later, Groucho commented to me that he felt it was probably the finest book to date on the team. I can't take all the credit — after all, the material was there years before I was born. It only needed to be transferred from celluloid to paper. That was accomplished by spending long hours over a movieola and light box and inducing ulcers in the still departments of Universal and MGM. The same process was duplicated for this volume.

Just as you, I too have some favorite scenes from W. C. Fields' films. Yet, with forty films from which to choose, you can readily understand that somewhere along the line one of your favorites (and mine) will invariably be omitted. Forgive me these omissions, for there are reasons. First, I asked the designers to set

up the book to facilitate easy reading. I didn't want the book to be cluttered and hoped to have it flow along much like Fields himself. This meant using more space for fewer scenes but I feel the outcome justifies the means. Second, Fields' earlier work relied much more upon visual than verbal gags. This is not at all unusual when you recall that Fields began in silent films in 1915. In compiling these books, I have come to realize the need to have dialogue aid the reader in following a scene. Trying to carry too many pages of visuals alone didn't work unless I could devote more space to the scene. Hence, I concentrated on those gags which also contained dialogue. For instance, the porch scene from IT'S A GIFT (1934): It is, probably, one of Fields' most perfect scenes and a testimonial to his artistry. On screen, it lasts about eighteen minutes.

Having been driven from his bed by his nagging wife, Fields decides to sleep on a swing hanging over the porch. Initially the swing collapses, but one disturbance after another assures that Fields will have little or no

sleep. Unfortunately, I had to limit the scene to one confrontation, the famous Mr. LaFong bit. The rest of the scene involves milk bottles rattling, a coconut rolling down the stairs, Baby LeRoy throwing grapes onto Fields' nose through a knothole, and a couple of women yakking up a storm. All too visual to be completely captured in this format of limited space. There is no doubt that it could be done, but I couldn't justify using fifty pages or so just to illustrate one scene from one film. Hopefully, one day, an expansion of this format will allow me to do an entire volume on a single film.

As you flip through this book, you will notice that the pictures are a bit grainy. Remember that you are looking at frame blow-ups. All of these photos were blown up from 35mm frames and taken from the fine-grains in the vaults at Universal Studios. Using fine-grains insures an unusually good quality but there will always be a certain amount of fuzziness. The fuzziness is quite tolerable when one realizes that this material is just not avail-

able in any other format. Even the gray books (production stills) in the vaults do not hold 90% of the pictorial material found here. In fact, most of the gray books were filled with publicity stills, a good deal of which bore no resemblance to the films they were representing. The release of this book represents the publication of pictorial and script material never before available.

I don't expect these books ever to take the place of films. But until such time as the films become more easily available for home viewing, we will have to settle for sporadic film festivals and a book such as this. This book is merely designed for you to have fun while reflecting upon the aritistry of a truly great comedic mind.

I have always been one to criticize the current revival of older films at the expense of making theaters available to new product. With distribution as it is in America, the new film-maker needs all the encouragement he can get. But when he finds that he cannot place his film because an exhibitor would rather play it safe with a tried and true Fields film, it can be quite frustrating. Yet, if I have learned anything from repeated viewings of these acknowledged classics, it is to respect the earnestness with which these films were produced. Obviously, everyone cared for what they were creating. The lighting is excellent and each scene is calculated to move you further into the plot, no matter how trivial. The actors seem dedicated to making it all work and the directors were more concerned with telling a story rather than hoping that the audience would leave the theater marvelling about some intricate shot. I don't agree with those critics who bury their heads in the past trying to find the real Hollywood, nor can I appreciate those film-makers currently trying to reproduce the past. I do see that the past can teach us a great deal in enabling us to form an appreciation of an art which began as an industry where talented people just got together to do something for fun and in which they believed.

Fewer and fewer talented people have the opportunity to produce films in America because of the outdated values of the major American studios. During this latest stay in Hollywood I found most studios devoid of activity and most personnel anxiously awaiting the word from the networks as to what series would be retained for another year. Of the features shooting, one is able to discern the recklessness of present studio management. One extravaganza has an eight-million dollar budget. For that same money, 16 or more features could be sensibly produced by young and old talent, but the studios would rather bank on an old hat producer with an old hat theme than break out of a rut which has spelled disaster during the last decade. By the time I left that city, I had a pretty dim view of things as they will be over the next year or so. Each studio was looking for "a happy picture" or a mafia (bite my tongue) story to grind out, hoping that an old formula would assure future financial success.

Until some new wave takes over the American cinema, we will have to content ourselves with the few and far between gems that shine amidst the muck and rejoice that we will have the likes of a W. C. Fields to fall back upon during leaner days.

—Richard J. Anobile, August, 1972

ACKNOWLEDGEMENTS

It is only after completion of a project such as this that I can look back over the months and realize how many people lent a helping hand. Every time I set out on one of these books, I arrive all by my lonesome at the studio and in no time I find that I have developed a small army of people who, besides carrying out their normal studio duties, add my project to their burden. It is these people to whom I would like to express my appreciation and thanks.

They include Herb Stern and Jim Fiedler in the Universal Law Department. They helped clear the rights and the way through studio red tape. Chuck Silvers over at Universal Editorial probably caught the brunt of my harassment. He was the guy who made sure all the films I was to view were available, as well as screening rooms, movieolas and editing rooms and anything my little heart desired. Not only did he make sure I had everything I required, but he concerned himself with all aspects of the project and for this I will always be grateful. When Chuck was not around, I had Jim Vogel of Editorial to bother. While I was busy playing creator, Jim handled all the technical ends to insure that I didn't fall off my cloud.

After all the selections had been made, it was then a matter of transferring my grease marks to the frames on the fine grains. Wally Weber and his negative cutters did one helluva job in this area.

The Universal Still Department did a tremendous job. They took all the frames, kept them in numerical sequence and turned out negatives and prints on a daily basis. My thanks to Frank Roach, Francisco Amadur, Michael Chacon, Bob Lewis and Michael Mustain.

As for the distinctive design of this book I have Harry Chester's design studio to thank, with a special mention for Alex Soma who labored long and hard over this book. Aside from bringing a talent for creative design to this book, Alex also brought a unique knowledge of the films. Thank you, Alex.

There is a sad footnote to all of this. Grant Hough, who headed the Universal Still Department and with whom I worked throughout my two-month stay at Universal, passed away shortly after my return to New York. Grant worked hard to keep high technical standards throughout this project. His personal recollections of Fields (with whom he shared a few snorts) gave me a greater insight into my subject and enabled us to pass some pleasant hours. Grant Hough was a good man and an expert in his field. He will be missed.

—Richard J. Anobile.

Introduction

Judith Crist, noted film critic and author, regularly reviews movies for "TV Guide", "New York" Magazine, and NBC's "Today" TV show.

This is a redundancy. For certainly the ultimate tribute to W. C. Fields is that as the
years go by, now more than a quarter of a
century after his death, there is less and less
need for an "introduction" to his genius, let
alone the life and times of one of the greatest
natural humorists that America has been
heir to.

The retrospect and the perspective are,
however, constant enrichments for our appreciation of his art and the legacy of some
forty films that preserved it. True apprecia-
ation of Fields comes to some of us instinct-
tively and to others with experience and with
maturity; he was that rare comedian who is
not superficially "accessible" to all comers in
the guise of lovable tramp, cross-eyed buffoon
or spastic clown. The complexity of his character and of the comedy that sprang there-
from bear minute analysis — and that, you
will discover, is what this book is all about.

Fields in essence was an American Falstaff
at war with the twentieth century and its total
Establishment, an aged-in-the-cask Gargan-
tua trapped in middle-class morality, an alter
ego for all of us in our daily frustrations, our
petty rages, our dishonesties and our dreams
of glory, superhuman in his survivals and
human enough to touch the heart — just a
little — after pounding the funnybone. He was
anti-Establishment before the phrase became
facile, but he opposed it right from the middle,
the white-collar man at war with all the social
machinery that entraps the middle class, from
foul family life to professional persecutions,
from doctors, lawyers and bankers to the abom-

inations of just-folks folks, particularly the children among them. His comedy was black before the fashion came, and he was the ultimate anti-hero before the armpit-scratching slouchers took over the role, the totally unregenerate fraud who mouthed the pomposities and mumbled the insults and conned his way in and out of disaster with a carny's assurance that a fraud can triumph in a fraudulent world. He was Mr. Middle America, the poseur, the pitchman, the Falstaffian fake full of asides and alibis at home — but at home and in command everywhere *but* at home. As who among us is not?

With the born-yesterday perspective that each generation claims, we find Fields curiously avant garde in retrospect, but then, what genius is not? After all, he bestrode a half-century of American entertainment like a Colossus, from the music halls and vaudeville stages of the Nineties to the turn-of-the-century tour circuits to the Broadway stages of the 'teens and Twenties, to Hollywood of the Thirties and Forties, to radio — and had he not died at sixty-seven in 1946, he would have gone on without doubt to become one of the early greats of television. He was a vaudeville headliner at nineteen, his master juggling turn a "dumb" act (without commentary or patter and therefore eligible for international tours without language difficulty) that led to Royal Command performances and world-wide acclaim.

He made his first movie at thirty-six, immortalizing his pool-game routine in "Pool Sharks" in 1915, and continued to make silent films (among them "Sally of the Sawdust" and "That Royle Girl" for D. W. Griffith) while wowing Broadwayites in The Ziegfeld Follies for six years, George White's Scandals and his smash hit, "Poppy," the source of "Sally of the Sawdust" and of a far more successful remake in 1936, as "Poppy," with Fields' root character, the conniving Professor Eustace McGargle (super-salesman of talking dog- and doer-in of country bumpkins) in full voice. The "dumb act" and the silent Fields

14

(usually adorned with a fake mustache) had departed en route (Fields settled in Hollywood in the mid-Twenties) and the double-dealing double voice — bombastic and booming for the fraud, a mumbling adenoidal drawl for the inner man aware that there are no honest men to be cheated and that only suckers get even breaks — had been established as part of the new whole humorist.

For Fields without voice, as his silent films attest, is an entirely different cup of comedy, a master pantomimist indeed — but largely appreciated by the talkie-generations, I suspect, because we "hear" that gravelly swoosh-and-slide of vocal-nasal chords, the rhythm of the circumlocutions that convert a hit on the head to "a crack on the noggin," accompany a gallant hand-kiss with "What symmetrical digits!" and do in an enemy with a "Michael Finn." He was, after all, the one comic star of silent films who came to talkies and conquered new worlds by talking.

At his best, he talked pure Fields — on screen and off. Like the true humorists — Chaplin, the Marx Brothers, Mae West, Jimmy Durante — he was a total personality on screen as well as off, capturing a facet of the American personality and holding it up against the structure of "normal" society in all its hypocritical moralities. Fields, however, drew blood because (like Miss West and Chaplin and Fred Allen and virtually no latter-day comedians with the exception of the brilliant Woody Allen) he did not "assume" his character but kept it to himself; he did not put it in the hands of others but provided his own materials. He took over the screenwriters' creations by sheer force of personality (and mastery of the ad lib in excelsis), but he was in his finest flower as his own writer (a euphemism, really, since Fields' "screenplays" and "stories" were jots and scribbles on the backs of envelopes and whatever came to mind on the set). His best early work, four shorts for Mack Sennett ("The Dentist," "The Fatal Glass of Beer," "The Pharmacist" and "The Barber Shop," in

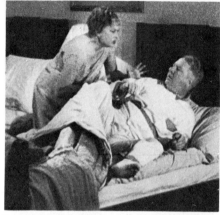

1932) were "original screenplays" by W. C. Fields, a name he used again in collaboration with Mae West for "My Little Chickadee" in 1940. It was as Charles Bogle (a long "o," he insisted) that he supplied the original story for "The Old-Fashioned Way" and "It's a Gift" (with J. P. McEvoy) in 1934, "The Man on the Flying Trapeze" in 1935 and "You Can't Cheat an Honest Man" in 1939. As Mahatma Kane Jeeves he provided both story and screenplay for what indeed stands as a classic of pure Fields as well as a classic American screen comedy, "The Bank Dick," in 1940, and in 1941 he provided the original story for "Never Give a Sucker an Even Break" as Otis Cublecoblis (pronunciation unspecified).

Consider the quintessentials of Fields' comedy in "The Bank Dick," wherein his Egbert Souse (accent grave on the "e" of course) is an improvident citizen of Lompoc saddled with a houseful of repulsive women (mother-in-law, wife and two daughters whose mouths are filled with food and/or venom); his major worry is that he might have lost twenty dollars the night before instead of spending it in the Black Pussy Cafe. As he's loafing, an escaping bank robber stumbles over him and is knocked cold; Souse claims credit for the capture and is rewarded with a job as bank dick. This enables him to proceed with a scheme to get his prospective son-in-law, a bank teller, to embezzle $500 to invest in a phony beefsteak mine, a scheme that involves zonking out a bank examiner; disaster looms but Souse, again inadvertently, gets involved in a second robber's getaway and wins not only a reward but is handsomely paid for a screenplay he managed to peddle to a visiting movie company (while taking over briefly for its drunken director); the beefsteak mine proves a goldmine as well. And Souse, at fade-out time, is a hero abroad and in his lavish new home where his fawning wife urges upon him a "second noggin of cafe baba au rhum." And in the course of this 74-minute virtually one-man show (although such fine comics as

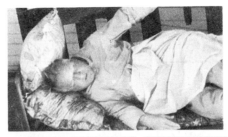

Franklin Pangborn, Cora Witherspoon, Una Merkel and Shemp Howard are on hand) Fields has managed to vent his spleen on women, children, directors, producers, actors, doctors, bankers and even little old ladies while proving himself a fraud, a phoney, a cowardly nebbish, a pompous lecher and a fool — all with the grace and style of the mahatmas of the world! And he's managed to touch base with all of us because we know what it's like in the Lompocs of this land and touched upon all our frustrations (whether it's the bank-teller's window closing in our face or finding the grapes we munch on are made of plastic) and given us a taste of fraudulence paying off in the way of this fraudulent world.

Fields is not likeable. Children with half a wit to see (whether it's the boot in Baby Leroy's behind or the urn about to be cracked on his daughter's noggin or his deft theft of the baloney from the sandwich he's to share with his son) can see nothing loveable there. And misogyny is rampant, along with the long underwear, bulgy belly and bulbous nose: Eddie Sutherland, who directed nine Fields films said the comedian missed super-stardom because women did not like him. Pauline Kael agrees, declaring that "For women, he is an acquired taste — like sour-mash bourbon. But then," she advises her sisters, "you can't go on sipping daiquiris forever." But from a purely humanistic point of view, as one examines the structures and details of the work of this angry artist—a man made paranoid by the early hardships of his struggle for success and by success itself, a Horatio Alger hero who refused to turn mealy-mouthed and forget and forgive just because he made it to the top — then indeed we find in Fields' art what Otis Ferguson rightly termed something "more real, more touching than the froth and fizzle of wit."

For Fields' is not the easy path of the pantomimist, or good "actor," equipped with glittering one-liners. His every move is choreographed, his total concept orchestrated. The

17

seeming rambling plotlessness (and consider, in the context of Hollywood slickeries of production and Mom-and-apple-pie-isms of the era, the courage of his producers in permitting him his free-form structures, let alone his iconoclasms) puts an aura of carelessness on his work. But Fields knew — from those first vaudeville moments and the disciplines of his primary art as a juggler — that there is structure and expansion as the base of comedic entertainment. There is the situation and the joke — but one laugh is not enough, just as a one-liner is inadequate. His genius was that each of his classic moments, as this book shows through sequential frames, builds from funny to funnier to funniest.

In this "Bullitt"-imitating era, there is still not a car chase to build in thrill or comedic effect quite the way the car chase in "The Bank Dick" did three decades earlier. Not since has anyone prepared with more hilarious sloth to respond to his wife's plea to rout singing burglars from the cellar as Fields does in "The Man in the Flying Trapeze" or suffered more relentless an assault from an insurance salesman than our sleep-starved hero in "It's a Gift." The building of the ballad of his son's tragic fate in "The Fatal Glass of Beer" on Fields' apology to his listener for "playing my zither with my mittens on"; the debacle of the poker game wherein our man has dealt himself five aces and draws nothing but aces thereafter; the glorious prelude to blowing the head off an ice cream soda. . . .

These are but a few of my favorite flowers of the Fields' creativity. There are others for you to savor and to study. "The funniest thing about comedy," Fields once wrote, "is that you never know why people laugh. I know *what* makes them laugh but trying to get your hands on the *why* of it is like trying to pick an eel out of a tub of water." Ours indeed not to reason why in the face of that. But the "what" is yours to find in the following pages, with all the joys of discovery — or of revisiting past pleasures.

Paramount
PRESENTS
TILLIE AND GUS
WITH
W. C. Fields, Alison Skipworth
and Baby LeRoy
Directed by FRANCIS MARTIN
COPYRIGHT MCMXXXIII by PARAMOUNT PRODUCTIONS, INC.
ALL RIGHTS RESERVED

**The trial is set and
Gus Winterbottom (Fields)
is the defendant.**

Judge: The defendant will take the stand.

Judge: I suppose you're acquainted with the penalty for perjury?

Gus: I object!

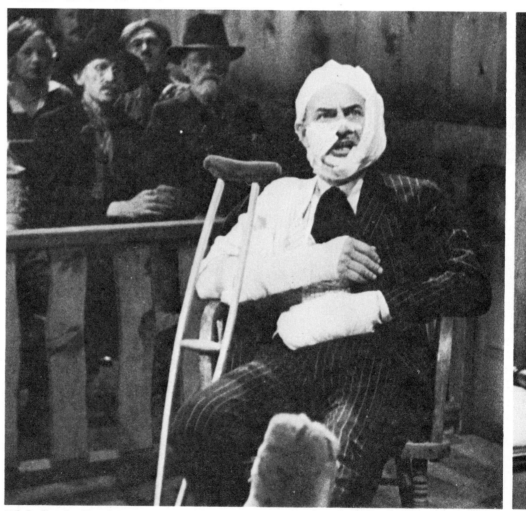

High-Card: Six shots!

Judge: Objection over-ruled! Sit down! Gus, you are hereby charged with pumping a load of lead into the anatomy of one High-Card Harrington.

Judge: Six hits!

Gus: Six cigars!

Gus: You shoulda worn your goloshes.

Judge: Have you anything more to say before I find you guilty?

Gus: So you're goin' to deal from a cold deck, eh?

Gus: Boys, this mummy . . . sitting over here inveigled me into a game of chance entitled . . . . . . draw poker. I figured right from the start I'd have to shoot him. It was all I could do to take his money!

Gus: Now listen, you — gentlemen of the jury . . . in this here game with High-Card, gents, I deals myself four aces, all regular.

What is my astonishment when High-Card there lays down five aces, against my four. I'm a broadminded man, gents. I don't object to nine aces in one deck, but when a man lays down five aces in one hand — !

And, besides, I know what I dealt him.

INTERNATIONAL HOUSE

Directed by
EDWARD SUTHERLAND

Having mistakenly landed his
"Spirit of Brooklyn" atop the roof garden of
the International House in WuHu, China, Professor
Quail (Fields) decides to orient himself.

Quail: Hey, where am I?

Peggy: Wu-Hu.

Quail: Wu-Hu to you, sweetheart! Hey, Charlie, where am !?

Manager: Wu-Hu.

Quail: Don't let the posy fool you.

Manager: This is the roof garden of the International House.

Quail: Where am I?

Quail: Never mind the details. What town is it?

Manager: This is Wu-Hu, China.

Quail: Then what am I doing here?

Manager: Well, how should I know?

Quail: Well, what is Wu-Hu doing where Kansas City ought to be?

Manager: Maybe you're lost.

Quail: Kansas City is lost; I am here!

Well, sweet buttercup? Now that
I'm here and see what's
to be had, I shall
dally in the valley,
and believe
me I can
dally.

Turn on those lights!

Turn on the lights. Give us lights.

Now can you
see anything?

Practically
everything.

What
won't they
think of
next?

Having dallied long enough, Professor Quail and socialite Peggy Hopkins Joyce decide to take leave of International House.

Quail: Here we are, my ravishing little pineapple. That wiggle of yours is becoming marvelous.

Peggy: I tell you I'm sitting on something.

Quail: You're sitting on something? Where are you, my little Mexican jumping bean?

Peggy: Where are you?

Quail: I'm up here in the fresh air. Come on up.

Peggy: Something's under me. What is it?

Quail: I don't know. I'll get down and investigate.

Quail: Uppsy-daisy.

Peggy: Ooooh!

Quail: Ah! It's a pussy! Worry not, my little titmouse, he has eight more lives to go. There you are, pussy. Run away now.

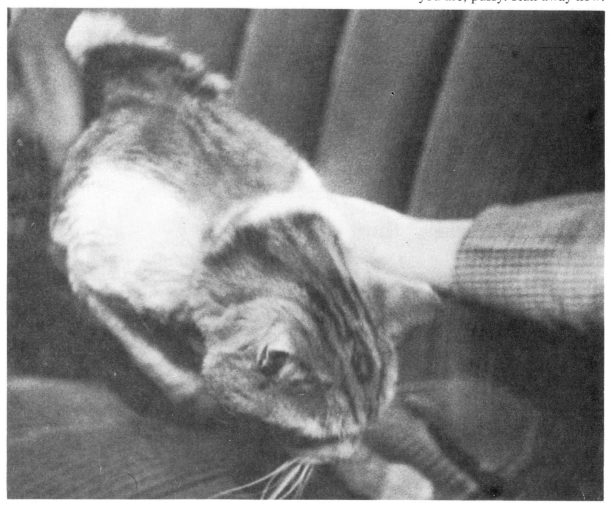

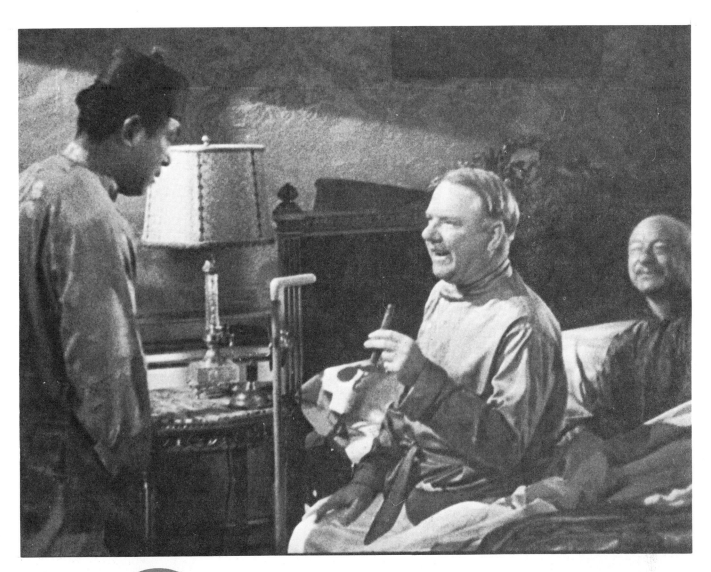

LATER

Quail: Get up my little cupcake.

Peggy: I'm sitting on something.

Quail: What again?

Peggy: Yes. I tell you, I'm sitting on something!

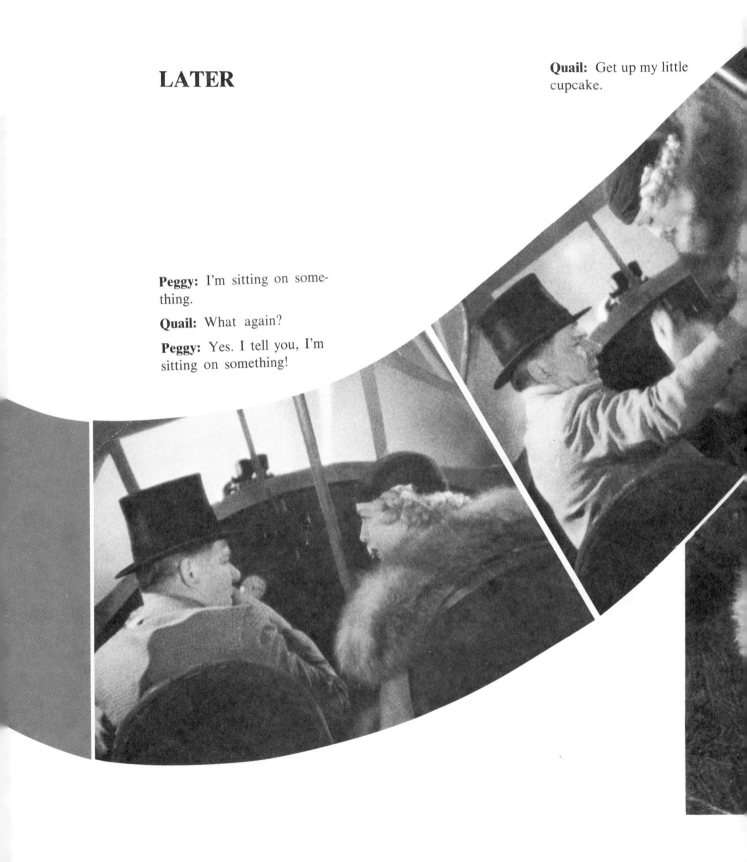

42

Peggy: I wonder what their their parents were?

Quail: Careless, my little nut cake, careless.

W. C. FIELDS
IN
You're Telling Me!
WITH
Larry "Buster" Crabbe, Joan Marsh
and Adrienne Ames
Directed by ERLE C. KENTON
COPYRIGHT MCMXXXIV by PARAMOUNT PRODUCTIONS INC.
ALL RIGHTS RESERVED

What with rumors around town to the effect that he has been carrying on with another woman, Fields seeks a way to make it up to his wife.

Doc: Why don't you take your wife home a present? A little pet of some kind. Women are crazy about pets.

Sam: They're just crazy. Pets haven't a thing to do with it.

Doc: Look at Charlie there.

Charlie: See what I'm taking home for the old lady.

Sam: It'll take a bigger bird than that to square me with my wife. Hey, pet man!

Sam: Whoa, Myrtle! Hey! Look out, Myrtle!

Fields regains his honor; the town regales Fields with an official visit.

Sam: Thank you. Mayor. You haven't a little dram on the hip, have you?

Mayor: Colonel, I always have a little something on the hip.

Sam: Mayor, you're okay. I voted for you last election — five times.

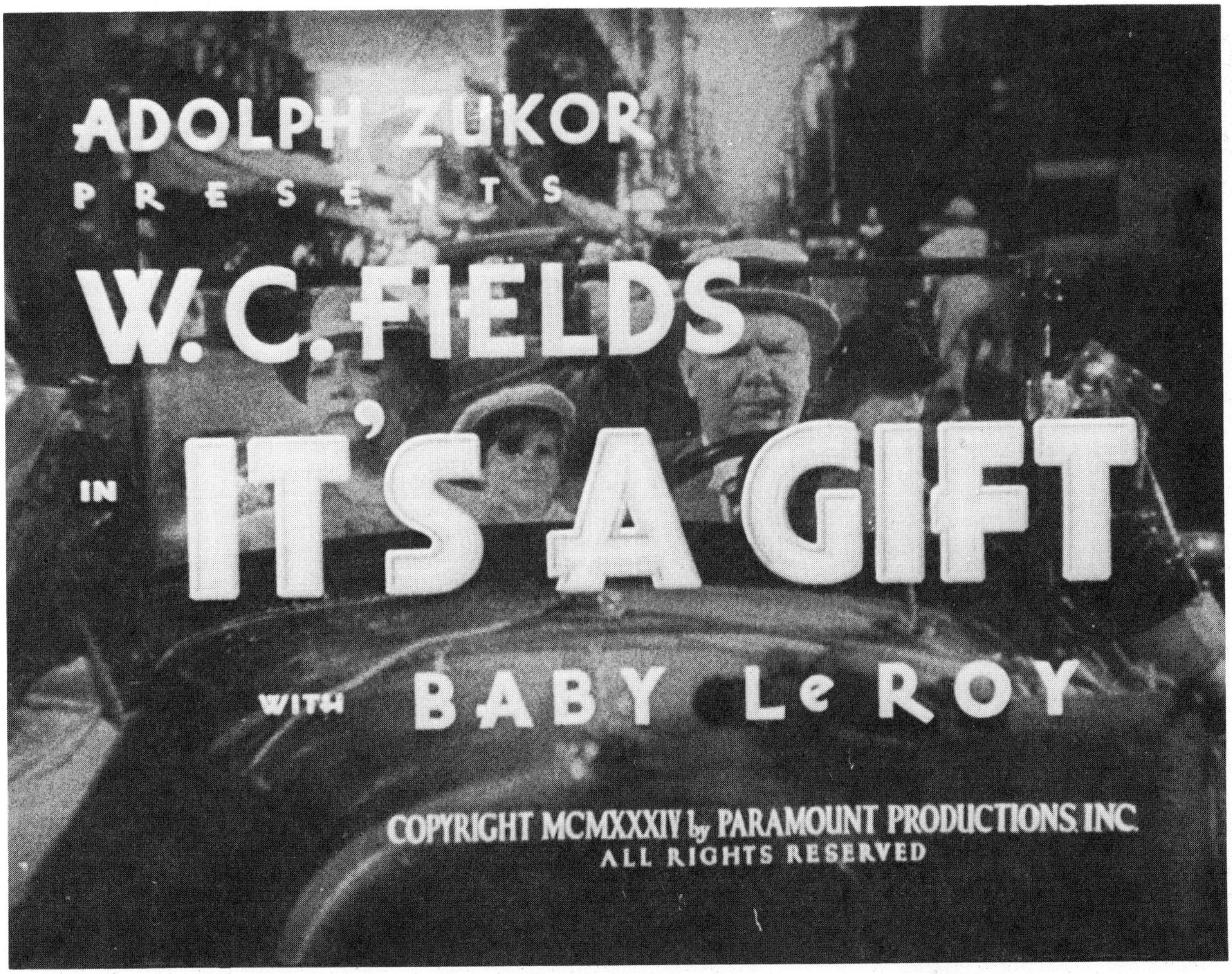
ADOLPH ZUKOR
PRESENTS
W.C. FIELDS
IN
IT'S A GIFT
WITH
BABY LeROY
COPYRIGHT MCMXXXIV by PARAMOUNT PRODUCTIONS, INC.
ALL RIGHTS RESERVED

Harold: Oh, it's the telephone. Shall **I** answer the telephone, dear?

Amelia: Naturally!

Harold: Yeah — naturally . . . naturally.

50

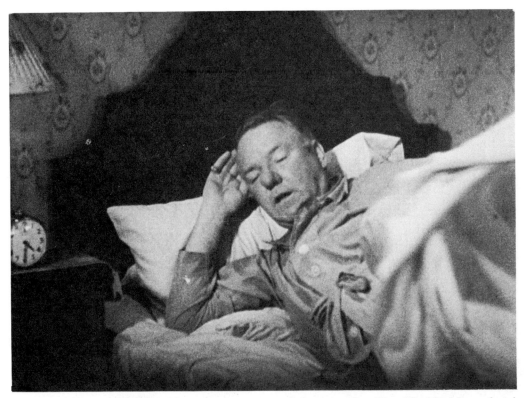

Harold: Ohh! **Amelia:** Oh, what are you doing now? **Harold:** Nothing, dear!

Harold: Can't think of the number.

Harold: Ohh — Hello, No. No. No, this is not the Maternity Hospital.

Harold: Think we ought to take that telephone out.

Amelia: Who was it?

Harold: Uh — somebody called up. Wanted to know if this was the Maternity Hospital.

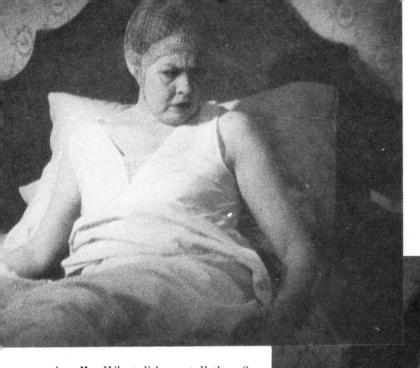

Amelia: What did you tell them?

Harold: Uh — I — I told 'em no,
it wasn't the Maternity Hospital.

Amelia: Funny thing they should
call you up here at this hour of
the night from the Maternity
Hospital.

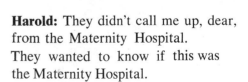

Harold: They didn't call me up, dear,
from the Maternity Hospital.
They wanted to know if this was
the Maternity Hospital.

Amelia: Oh! Now you change it!

Harold: No, I didn't change it, dear.
I told — I told you they — uh —
they asked me if this was the
Maternity Hospital.

Amelia: Don't! Oh, don't make it any worse.   **Harold:** They asked me —

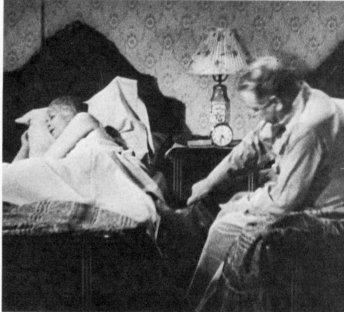

Amelia: I don't know how you expect anybody to get any sleep, hopping in and out of bed all night, tinkering around the house, waiting up for telephone calls.

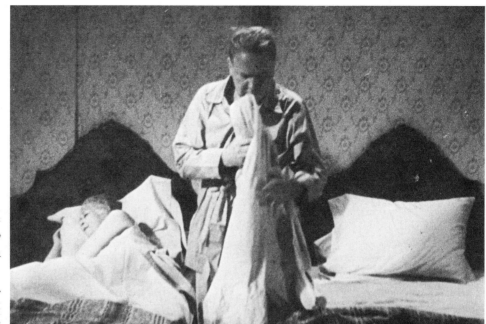

Amelia: You have absolutely no con sideration for anybody but yourself. I have to get up in the morning, get your breakfast for you and the children. I have no maid, you know — probably never shall have one.

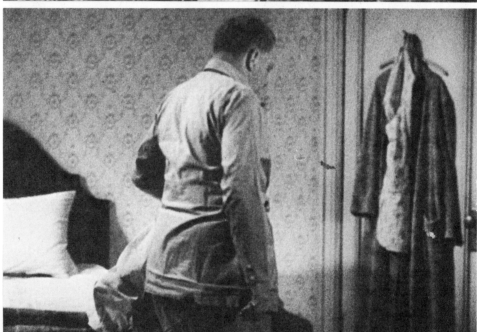

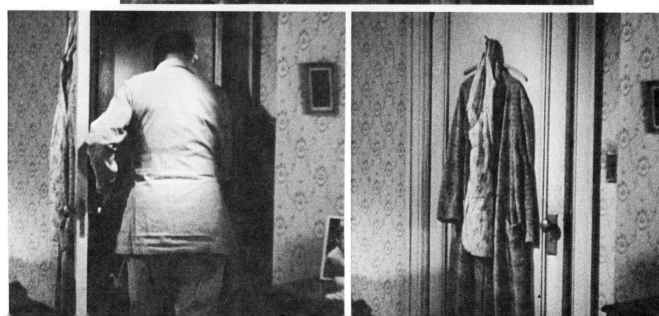

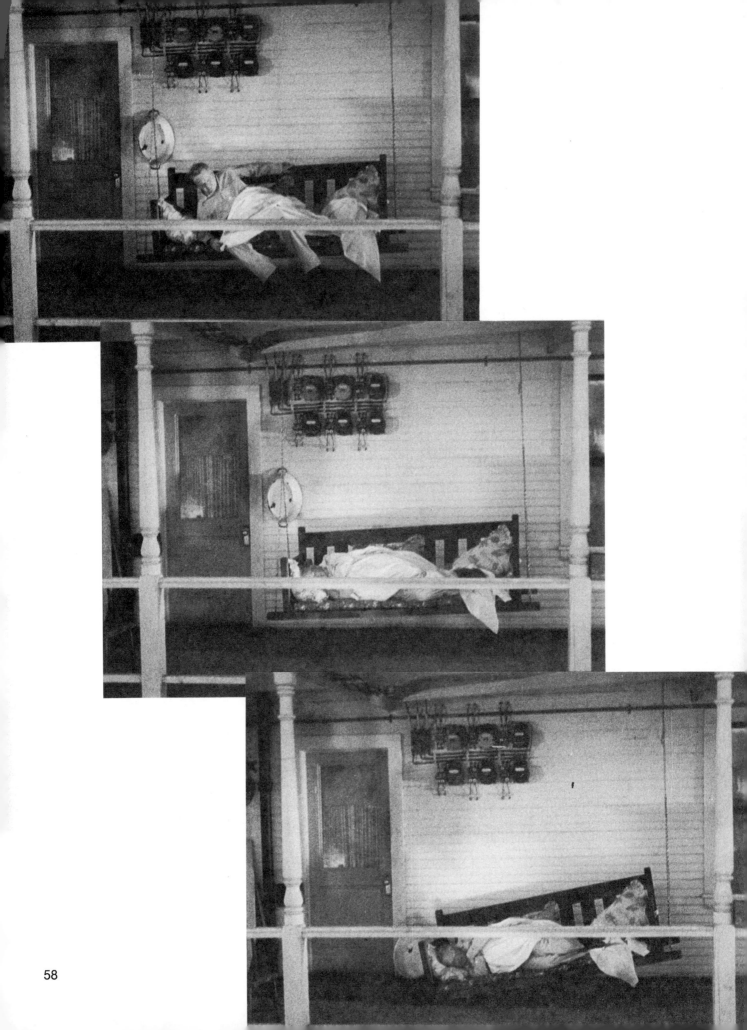

Amelia: Harold! Will you please keep quiet and let me get some sleep!

Harold: Coming, com —-Uh — yes, yes, dear. Yes.

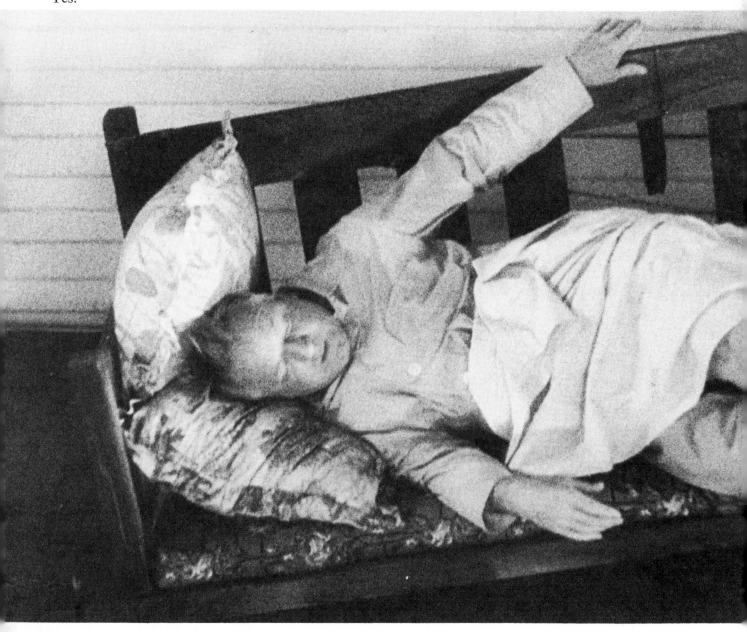

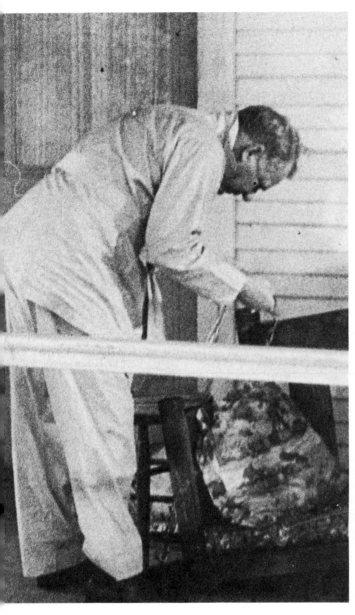

Harold: What a night! It was not a night for love!

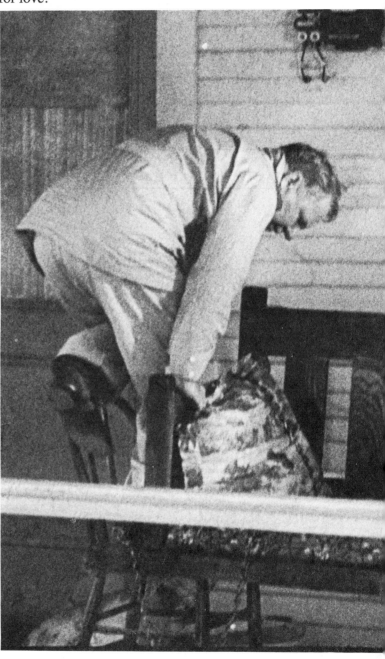

Agent: Is this seventeen-twenty-six Prill Avenue?   **Harold:** No.

Agent: Is there a Prill Avenue in
this neighborhood?

Harold: I don't know.

Agent: Do you know a man by the name of LaFong — Carl La Fong? Capital L, small a, Capital F, small o, small n, small g. LaFong. Carl LaFong.

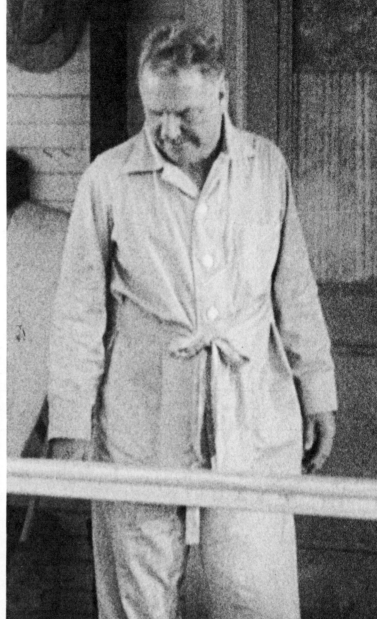

Harold: No, I don't know Carl LaFong — capital L, small a, capital F, small o, small n, small g! And if I did know Carl LaFong, I wouldn't admit it!

62

Agent: Well, he's a railroad man, and he leaves home very early in the morning.

Harold: Well, he's a chump.

Agent: I hear he's interested in an annuity policy.

Harold: Oh, isn't that wonderful!

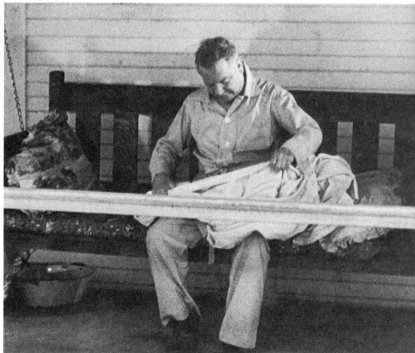

Agent: The public are buying them like hotcakes.   **Harold:** Oh!

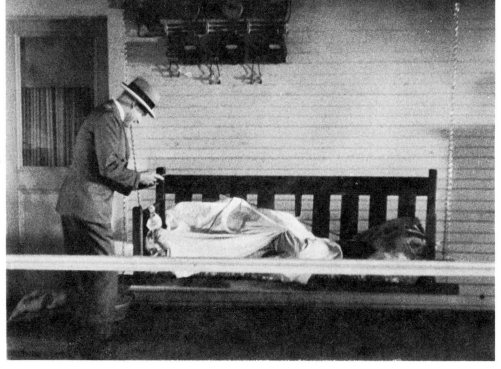

Agent: All companies are going to discontinue this form of policy after the twenty-third of this month.

Harold: That's rather unfortunate.

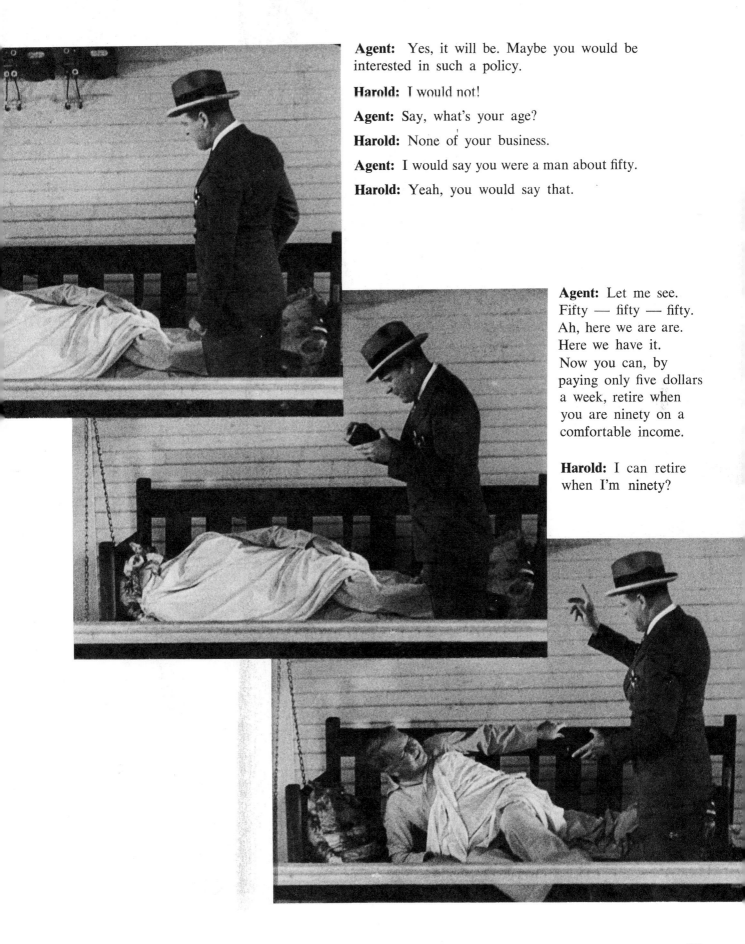

Agent: Yes, it will be. Maybe you would be interested in such a policy.

Harold: I would not!

Agent: Say, what's your age?

Harold: None of your business.

Agent: I would say you were a man about fifty.

Harold: Yeah, you would say that.

Agent: Let me see. Fifty — fifty — fifty. Ah, here we are are. Here we have it. Now you can, by paying only five dollars a week, retire when you are ninety on a comfortable income.

Harold: I can retire when I'm ninety?

Agent: That's right. You got the idea right the first time.

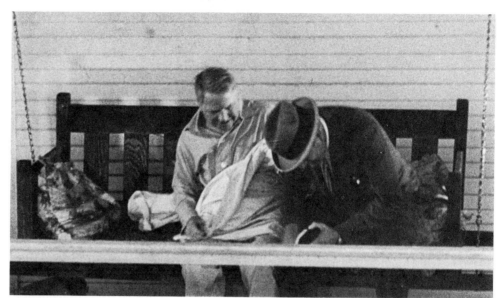

Harold: Look out! Don't sit down there.

Agent: Or you can change to a regular paid up policy —

Harold: Oh!

Agent: — and at death —

Amelia: Harold!

Agent: — your beneficiaries—

Amelia: Harold! If you
and your friend wish
to exchange ribald stories,
please take him downstairs!

Harold: My friend!·

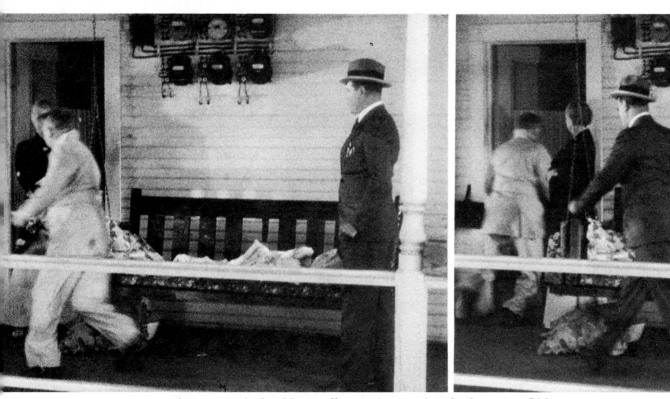

Agent: And should you live to be one hundred, we — Oh!

Harold: I suppose if I live to be two hundred, I get a velocipede!

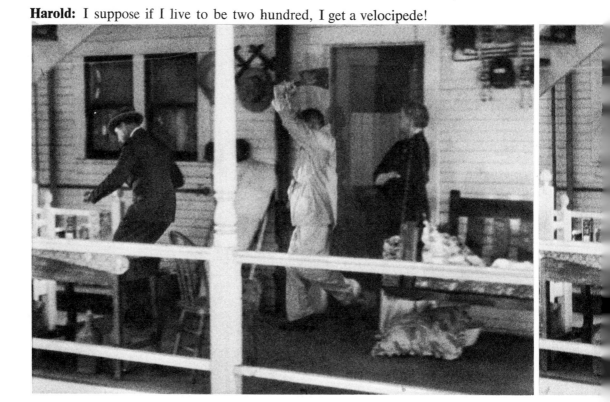

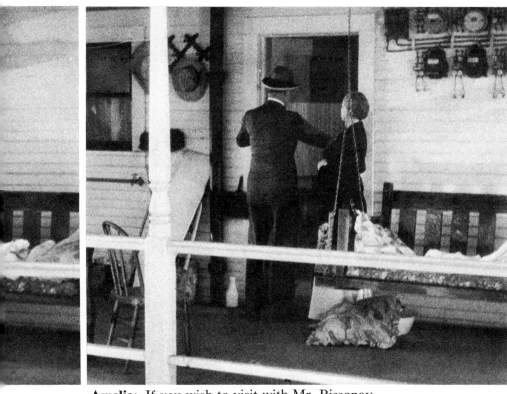

Amelia: If you wish to visit with Mr. Bissonay,
come around some morning, say about ten o'clock.

Harold: I never want to see him again!

Amelia: Then why did you invite him up here?   **Harold:** Huh!

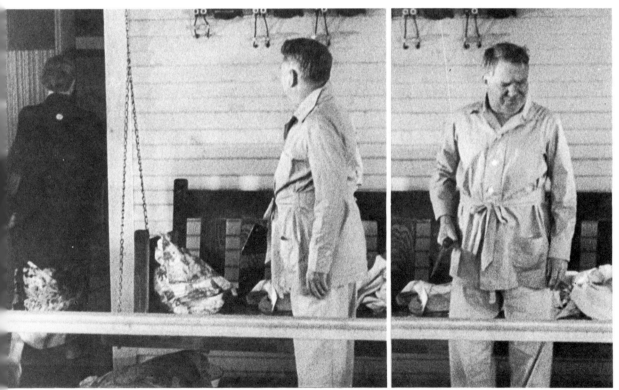

Harold: I invite. — I'd like to — Oh! Oh! Oh! Oh, if I could only retire now.

70

ADOLPH ZUKOR presents
W.C. Fields
in
MAN ON THE FLYING TRAPEZE
WITH MARY BRIAN
Produced by WILLIAM LeBARON
COPYRIGHT MCMXXXV by PARAMOUNT PRODUCTIONS, INC.
ALL RIGHTS RESERVED

Ambrose Woolfinger (Fields) is called upon in his role as man of the house.

Leona: Ambrose! Ambrose! Did you leave the radio on? Did you leave the radio on? Ohhh!

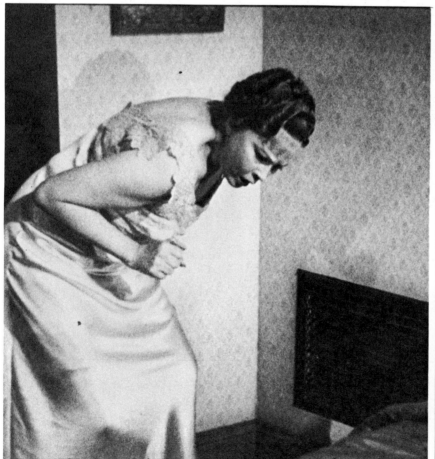

Leona: Ambrose! Ambrose! Wake up! Wake up.

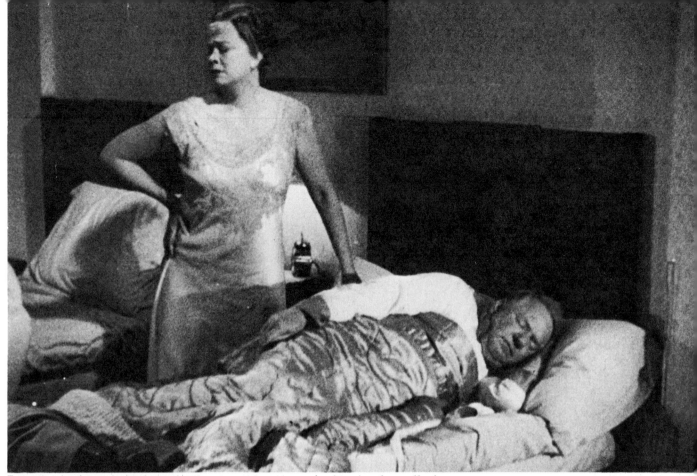

Leona: Ambrose! Ambrose! There are burglars singing in the cellar!

Ambrose: What?   **Leona:** There are burglars singing in the cellar!

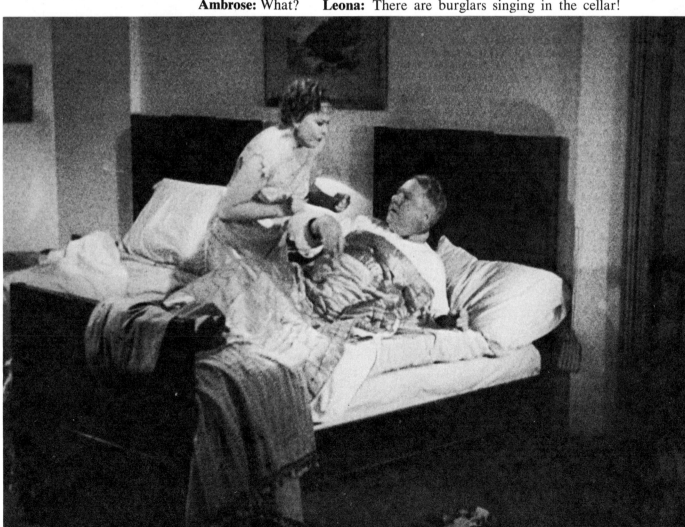

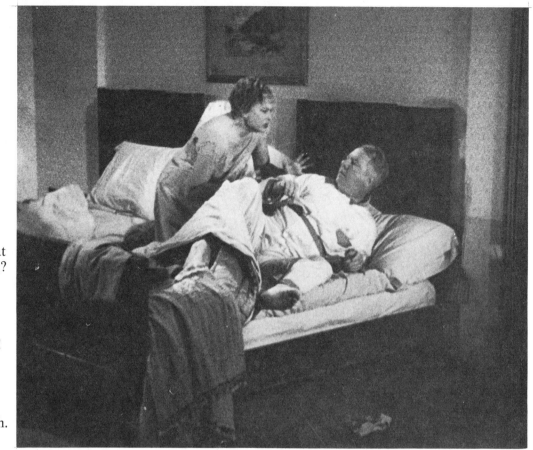

Ambrose: What are they singing?

Leona: What difference does it make what they're singing! Get up and see what it's all about.

Ambrose: Yeah. That's right.

Leona: Don't sit there like a bump on a stump! Go down and throw them out. Hurry! Hurry! Hurry, Ambrose, hurry!

Ambrose: What are they singing down there for?

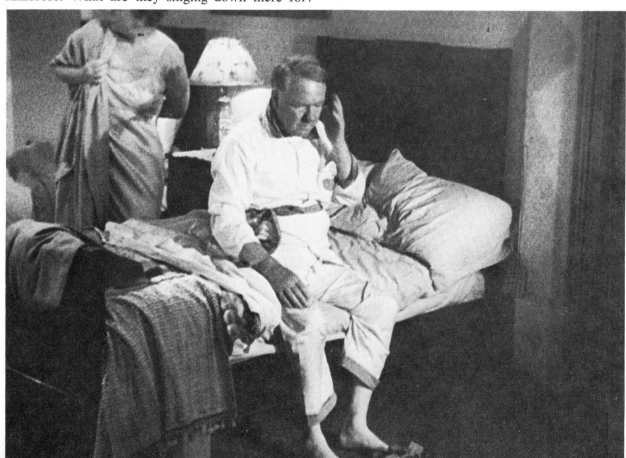

Leona: Well, it doesn't matter what they're singing. Go down quickly, Ambrose. We're in danger, I tell you. We're in terrific danger, Ambrose.

Ambrose: The more haste, the less, speed. I'll be down there.

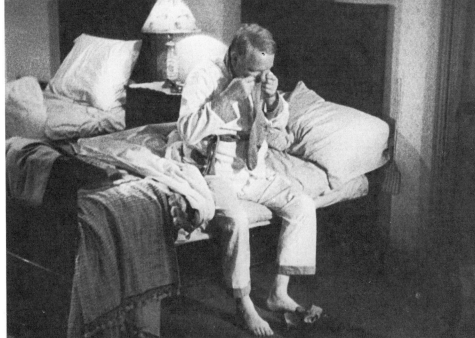

Leona: Oh, Ambrose, my poor Mother! My poor, helpless old Mother!

Ambrose: Umm.

Leona: My darling —

Ambrose: She's upstairs. They won't find her. She's up —

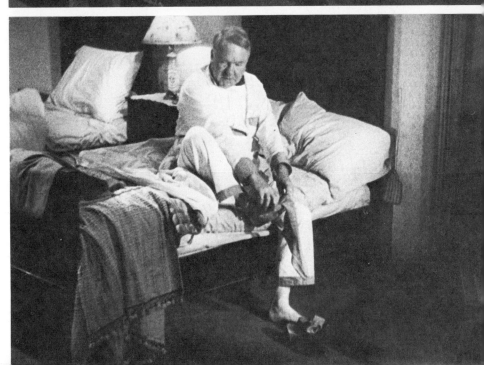

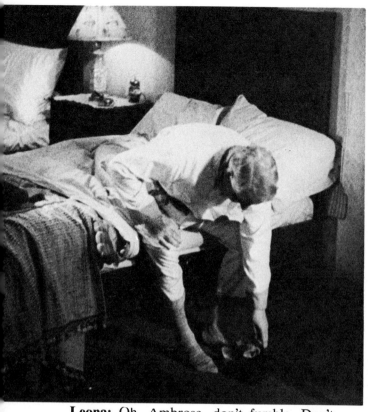

Leona: Oh, Ambrose, don't fumble. Don't fumble, Ambrose. Hurry, Ambrose, hurry.

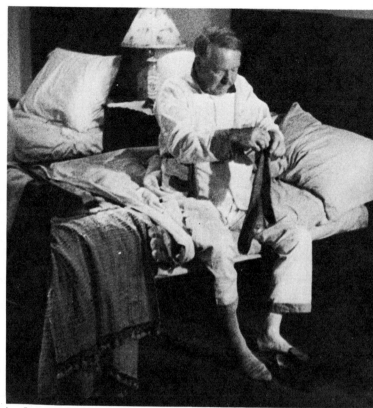

Ambrose: I'm coming, dear.

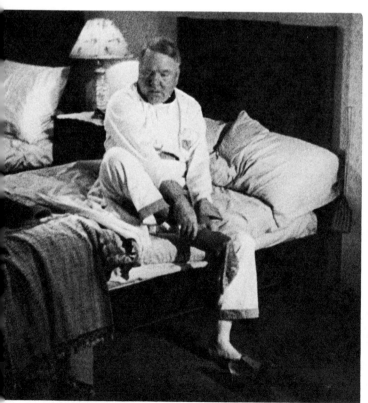

Leona: Oh, Ambrose, hurry! They're great murderers — brutes, They've got guns. Now what are you looking for, Ambrose!

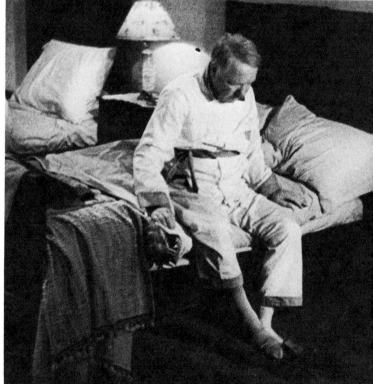

Ambrose: I don't know, they may not have guns.

Leona: Oh, Ambrose.

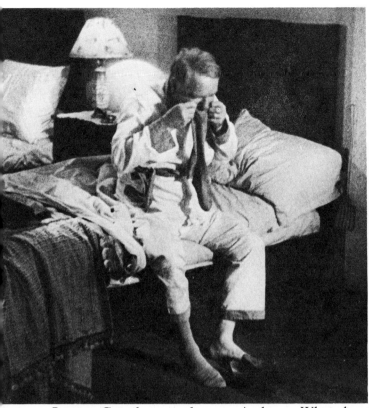 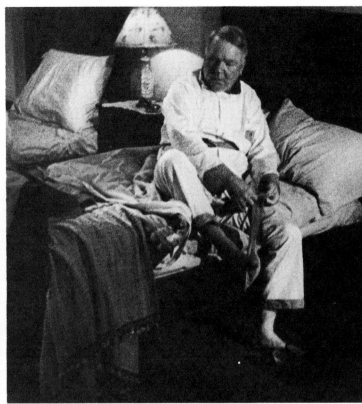

Leona: Get those socks on, Ambrose. What does it matter whether you've got your socks on or not?

Ambrose: I'll catch cold down there.

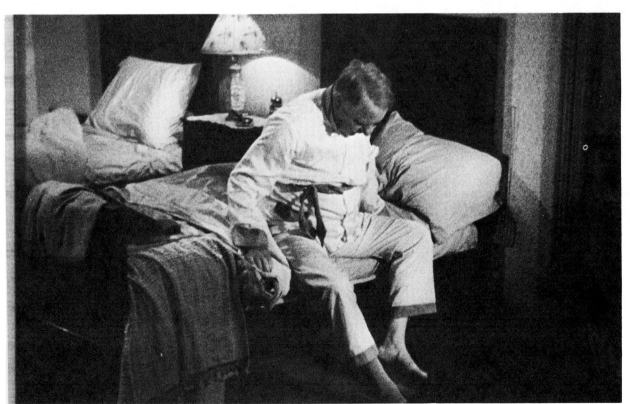

Ambrose: Maybe they mistook our cellar window for a stage door.

Leona: Hurry, Ambrose, hurry! It's getting louder, and louder, and louder.

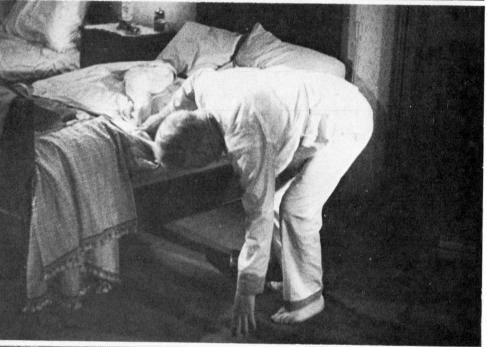

Ambrose: I can't find my socks. You're getting me so nervous, I've lost my socks.

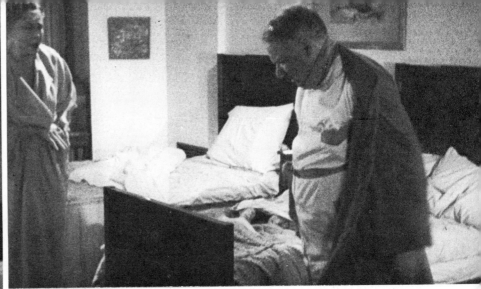

Leona: Oh, Ambrose, hurry! What are you looking for now?

Ambrose: Why couldn't they wait until later on in the morning?
Leona: Oh, hurry, Ambrose, hurry! Hurry!

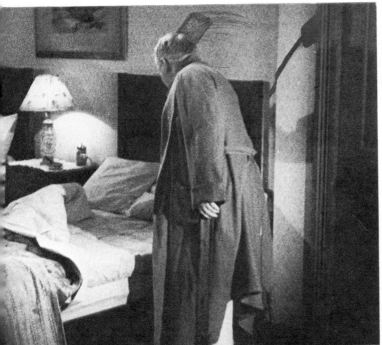

Leona: It's getting louder. It's getting louder! Hurry! Oh, don't swat flies! Hurry, Ambrose!

Ambrose: Huh?

Leona: Hurry!

Ambrose: Huh? Oh, such an earthly hour — an unearthly hour! Where are they?

Leona: In the cellar, Ambrose.
Ambrose: Oh.

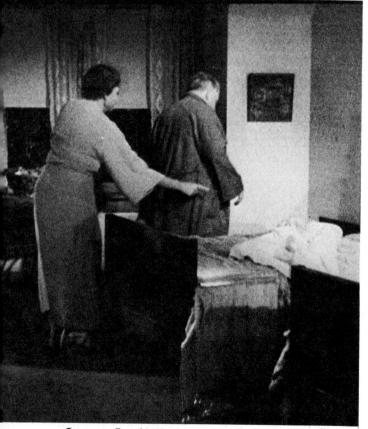

Leona: In the cellar! Listen, listen, listen!

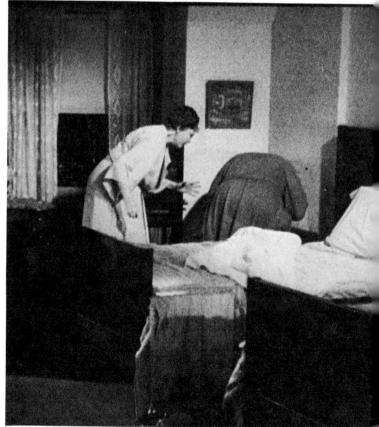

Ambrose: Oh, what rotten voices!

Leona: Oh, Ambrose, quick! Get them, Ambrose, get them!

Ambrose: Oh, gosh, couldn't I just sleep about another hour, then I'll go down after them.

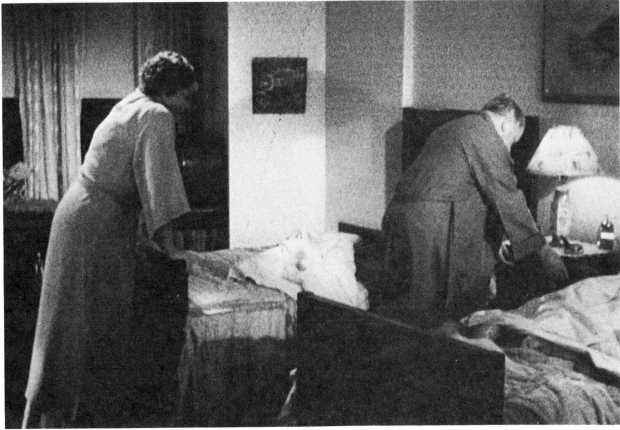

Leona: Oh, Ambrose, hurry. Hurry, Ambrose.

Ambrose: Okay. Oh, this is awful.

Ambrose: Look at that. There's the gloves that you lost two weeks ago.

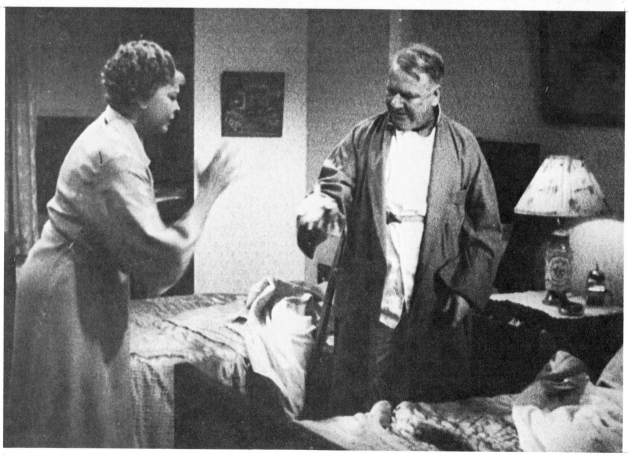

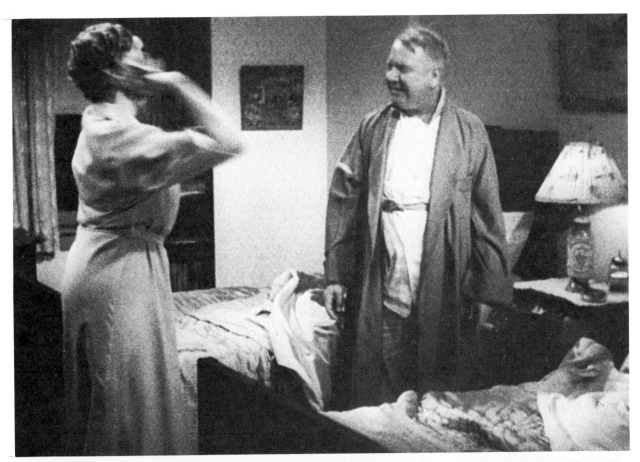

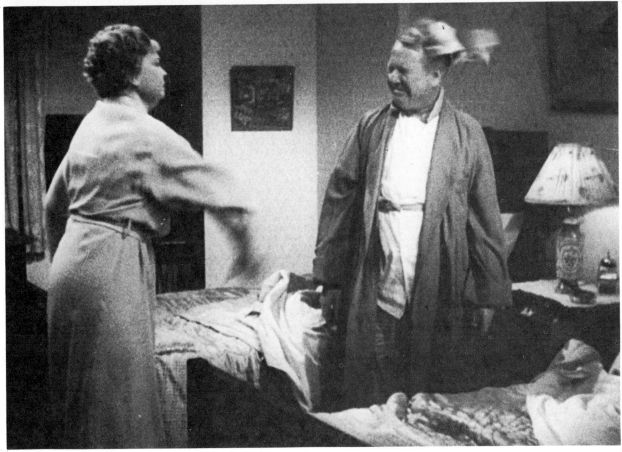

Leona: Oh! Ambrose, get the gun!

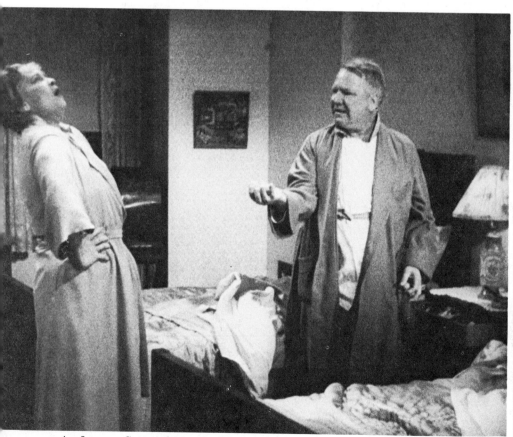

Ambrose: Say, what are these doing in here — all these walnuts?

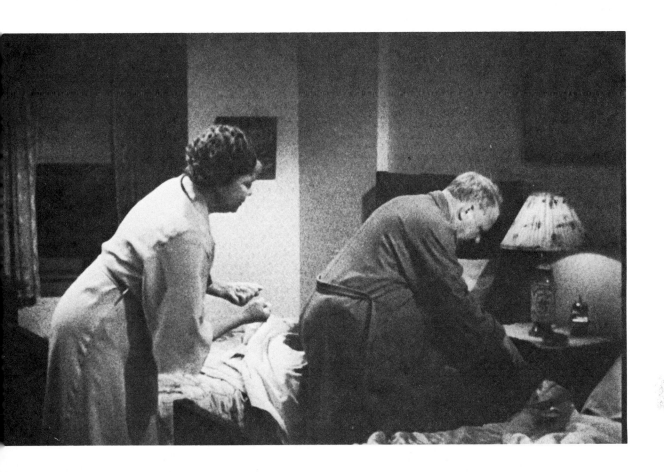

Leona: What's the difference what they're doing? Get the gun, Ambrose, get the gun!

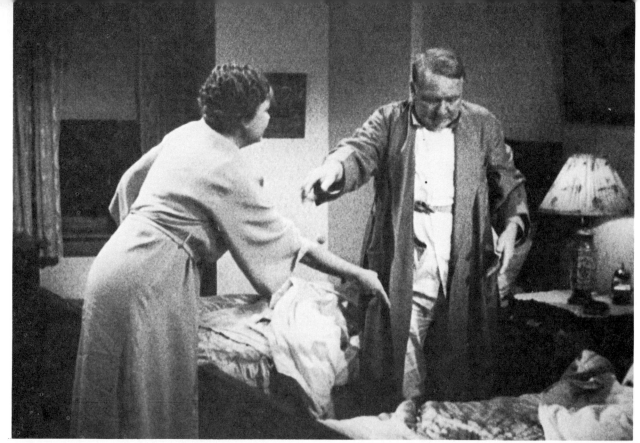

Ambrose: Uh look, there's nothing — there's no — Yes, here it is — here it is — I've got it. Here, I got it.
Leona: Be careful!

Ambrose: Oh, there's nothing to . . . be frightened of.

Leona: Be careful!

Ambrose: It's unloaded. There's nothing in it.

Leona: Careful!

Ambrose: It's okay. There isn't a bullet in it.

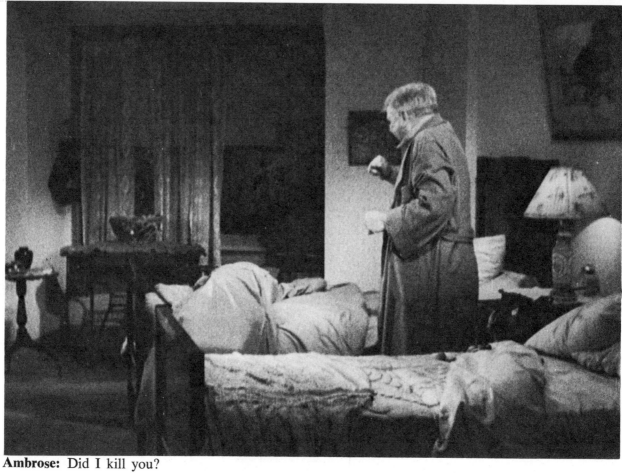

Ambrose: Did I kill you?

Leona: Oh, leave me in peace! Leave me in peace!

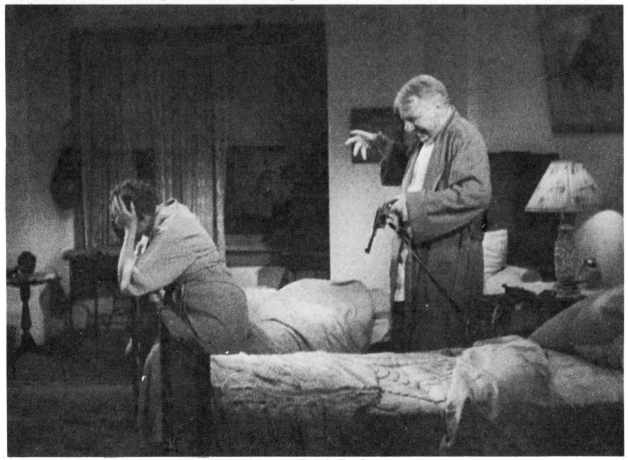

Ambrose: Good, good, good. I didn't kill you. That's fine!

Having apprehended the criminals there remains the task of escorting them to jail and explaining the problem to the law.

Ambrose: Keep quiet, boys. I don't want anybody to see me prowling around in the middle of the night dressed like this.

Berg: What time is it?

Legs: What time is it?

Willie: What time is it?

Man: Say, Woolfinger, what's the idea of making all this noise at five o'clock in the morning!

Ambrose: Uh — five o'clock.

Ambrose: Drat!

Ambrose: Say, this thing isn't going to interfere with me going to the wrastlin' match this afternoon, is it?

Berg: Oh, I hope not. I got a ticket myself.

Ambrose: I got a fifteen dollar seat in the first row.

Berg: Ummm!

Ambrose: Had it for three weeks. Of course my wife knows nothing about it. Wrastling's in my blood. You know if I hadn't of been sidetracked, I'd been probably wrastling in this match this afternoon myself.

Berg: Oh, you're a wrestler, eh?

Ambrose: You're born in Canada, weren't you?
Berg: Yes.

Ambrose: Fine. There isn't a man or boy born in the United States or Canada that could get out of this hold.

Ambrose: Come here. Stick your head in there. Stick it in there. Go ahead. Put it in there.

Ambrose: Now, wait a minute. Now. Try to get out of that. Yeah, try to get out of it

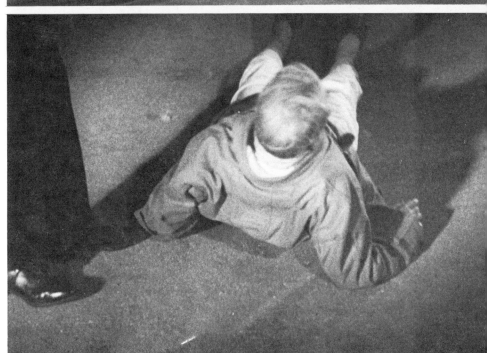

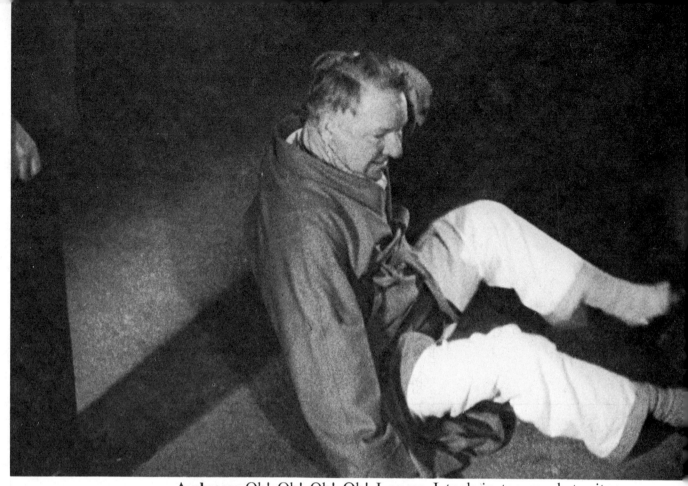

Ambrose: Oh! Oh! Oh! Oh! I guess I took in too much territory.

Berg: Did I hurt you?   **Ambrose:** How could you hurt anybody throwing them on their head?

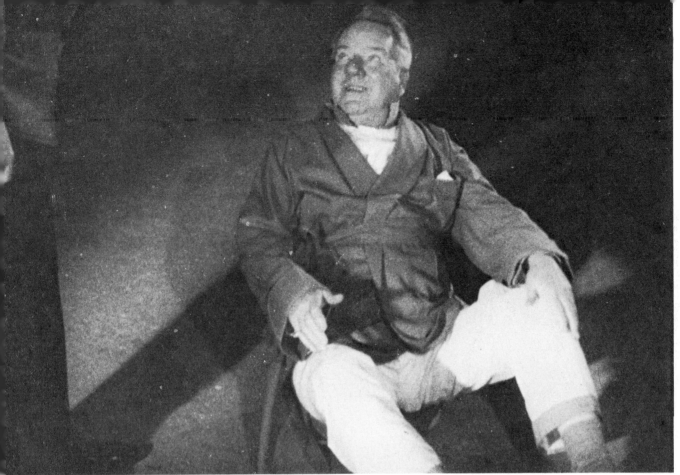

Ambrose: I shouldn't have mentioned Canada.

Ambrose: Oh, dear. Oh! Oh! Oh!

Judge: What's the charge?

Berg: Those two men, Your Honor, were singing in Mr. Woolfinger's cellar.

Ambrose: These two boys here.
Judge: Yes?

Berg: And drinking applejack.
Judge: Where'd they get it?

Berg: In Mr. Woolfinger's cellar.
Ambrose: Down at my place.

Judge: Where's the evidence?

Ambrose: Uh — right here, Your Honor.

Judge: Who's the owner of this applejack?

Ambrose: I am.

Judge: Have you a permit to manufacture applejack?

Ambrose: Uh— I beg your pardon?

Judge: Have you a permit to manufacture applejack?

Ambrose: Uh, I guess I could get one easy enough.

Judge: Thirty dollars or thirty days. Take him away.

Ambrose: These are the — these —

Berg: But, Judge —

Ambrose: They came in to my —

Judge: Clear the Court! Clear the Court!

Berg: Listen —

Ambrose: Oh, this is terrible!

Berg: This is awful! This is terrible!

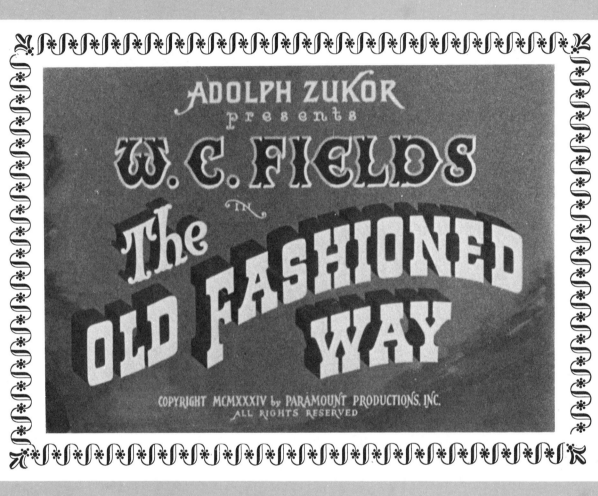

The Great McGonigle and his theatrical troupe sit down to enjoy a collective meal at their boarding house. It's Baby Leroy, however, who sets the tone of the meal.

Cleo: Oh, Mr. McGonigle, I'm so glad to see you. I've been so excited ever since I knew you were coming to town.

McGonigle: Ah! My dear Cleopatra Pepperday! How delighted I am to see you!

Cleo: Oh, Mr. McGonigle! I didn't think you'd remember me.

McGonigle: Remember you? How could I forget you? How could anyone forget you?

Cleo: Oh, Mr. McGonigle!

McGonigle: Will you sit down here?

Cleo: Oh, thank you.

103

McGonigle: Thank you, dear. It is a pleasure and an honor to have you sit at my right . . . to break bread with you on such a delightful afternoon.

Cleo: Thank you, Mr. McGonigle! Oh!

McGonigle: Oh, don't mention it.

McGonigle: Well, little man, do you know who I am?

Albert: Da-da.

McGonigle: No, you have me wrong.

Cleo: His name's Albert, after his dear, departed father.

McGonigle: Yes?

McGonigle: He has a wonderful . . . . . head. Ummm!

McGonigle: Shaped like a Rocky Ford cantaloupe.

McGonigle: Are we going to have him with us for dinner?

McGonigle:
Let me — let me
see. Now, come on
here. Come on.

McGonigle: He's
holding onto the
floor.

McGonigle: There we are. There we are. Look out! Here. I'm just going to help you in, that's all.

Cleo: He's such a friendly little man.

McGonigle: Yes, he is.

McGonigle: There you are. Get your foot over there. Oh-oh!

McGonigle: Where's his other — ? Can you see his other foot? Oh, here it is.

McGonigle: Yes, there you are. Now you're all right.

McGonigle: Now I have him. Ah! Oh, there you are.

Cleo: Oh, there you are! Now!

McGonigle: He has a mind of his own, hasn't he?

Cleo: Just like his father.

McGonigle: There you are. Look at that. There. Now, could anything be nicer than that?

McGonigle: Ooop! Ooops!

Cleo: Oh, Mr. McGonigle!

McGonigle: Now, come here.   **Cleo:** Ah!

McGonigle: There, little man.

Cleo: Oh, Mr. McGonigle! I do hope you let me sing for you this year. You know you were too busy when you were here last time.

McGonigle: Yes, we were very prosper - uh - very busy last season, yes.

Cleo: Umm, but you will let me sing for you this time?

McGonigle: I've been looking forward to it for months.

Cleo: Oh, thank you!

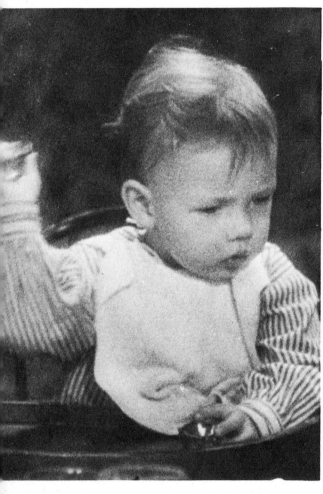

McGonigle:
Oh, really!

Cleo: Oh, Albert! Now, you shouldn't have done that! Whatever possessed you? Oh, Mr. McGonigle, I'm so sorry.

McGonigle: Very well done.

Albert: Da Da . . .

McGonigle: I don't know whether to eat from my coat or from my plate!

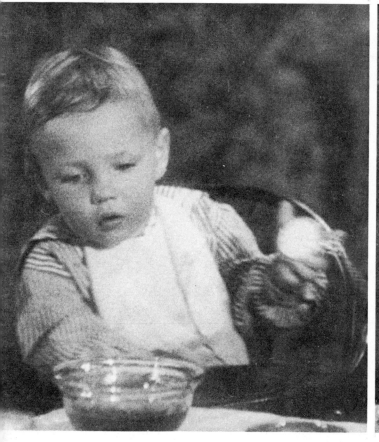

Cleo: Albert, look what you've done to Mr. McGonigle's watch! Oh!

Cleo: Oh, I'm so sorry! Oh, Mr. McGonigle!

McGonigle: Oh, it's all right.

Cleo: He's such an impulsive nature. Just like my own.

McGonigle: Don't apologize; It's all right. Just a little child, you know.

Cleo: Oh, he does the cutest things!

McGonigle: Yes, he does.

Cleo: I wish you'd see him when no one's around.

McGonigle: I'd like to catch him - uh - see him sometime when no one's around.

Cleo: Oh, Albert! What did you do?

116

McGonigle: Bet the minute hand won't be a bit of use after this.

Cleo: Oh, Mr. McGonigle, I hope he hasn't hurt your watch.

McGonigle: Oh, no. How could you hurt a watch by dipping it in molasses?

Cleo: Oh, he's never done that before.

McGonigle: Ummm. Well, I hope he doesn't do it again . . . not with this watch.

Cleo: Oh, Mr. McGonigle, I hope you won't dislike my little Albert!

McGonigle: It'll make me love the little nipper the more.

McGonigle:
He's a brat!
A brat!
A b-r-a-t - brat!

Cleo: Albert . . . you mustn't do that!
Naughty! Naughty!

McGonigle: Oh, it's all right. D-Don't apologize.
Yes. I'm used to that sort of thing. Yeah. We stage
folks get that all the time.

Bertha: Listen folks. There's one of them new-fangled horseless carriages coming!

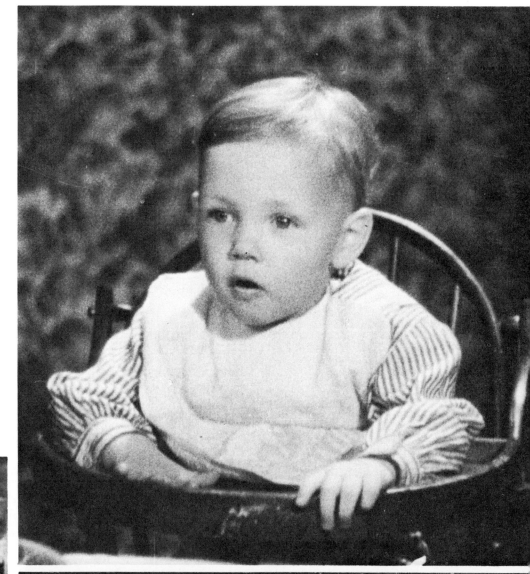

124

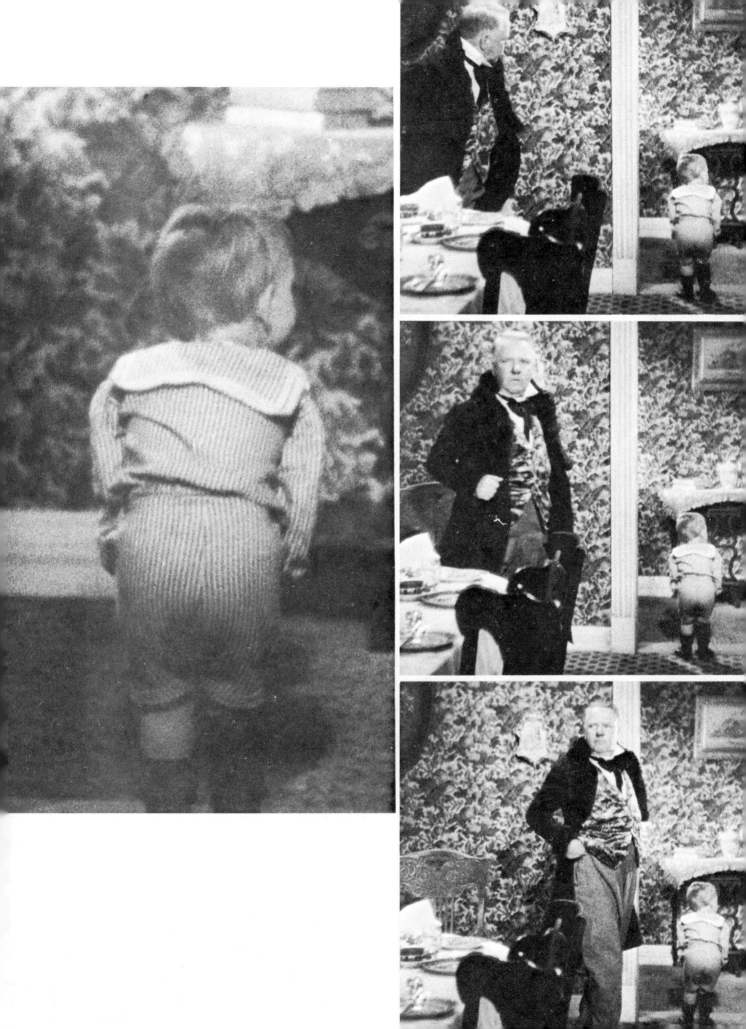

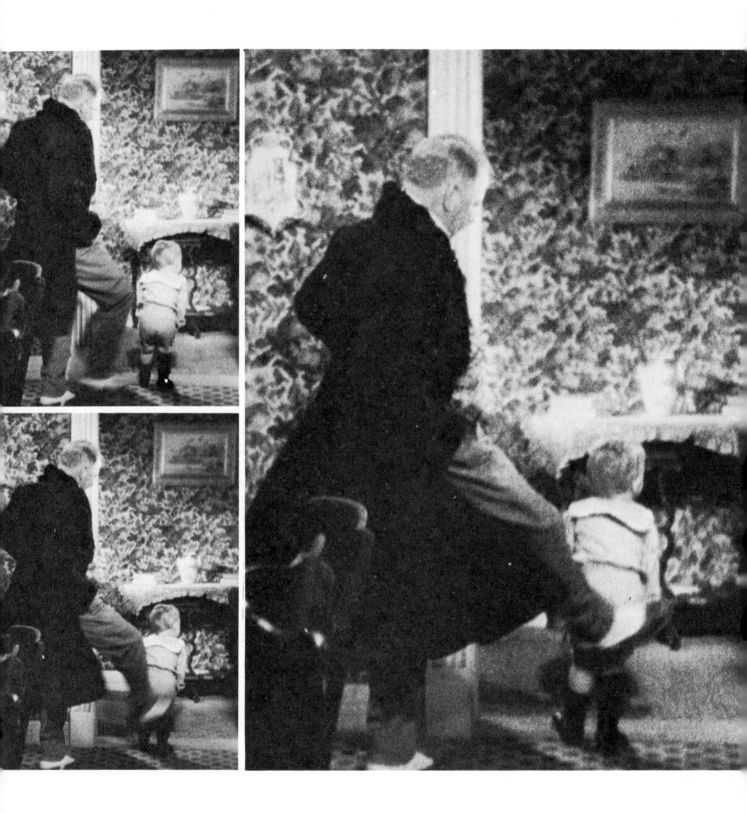

Tain't a fit night out for man or beast.

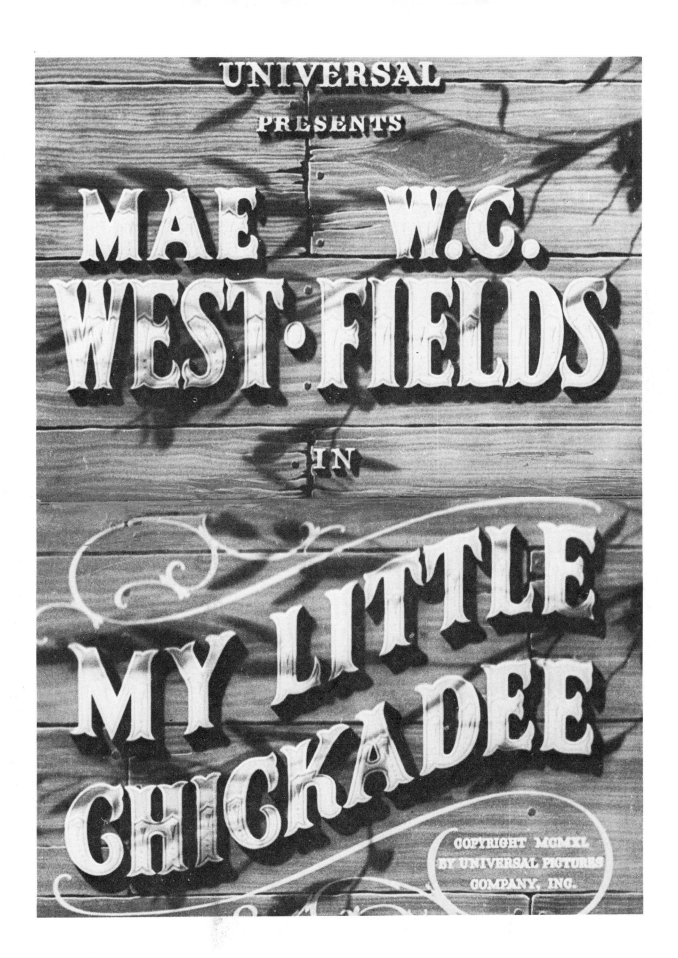

Cuthbert Twillie (Fields) shows us the fine art of hijacking a train and catching a girl in one move.

Indian: Hi!

Engineer: Hey — what are you doing down there?

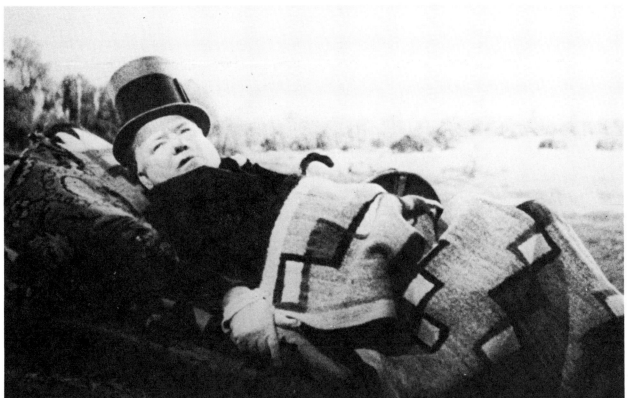

Twillie: Ah, how do you do, sir. Have you any private cars on this train? Room and bath with exclusive bar?

Engineer: No! Only day coaches.

Twillie: Drat! Allow me a half a tick to collect my portmanteau and some very valuable belongings and Milton, my lad — meet me at Greasewood City.

Indian: Ugh.

Twillie: Drat!

Mrs. Gideon: Did you break your umbrella?

Twillie: No. You can't break it. It's a genuine Chamberlain. Guess it's all right. There — that's better.

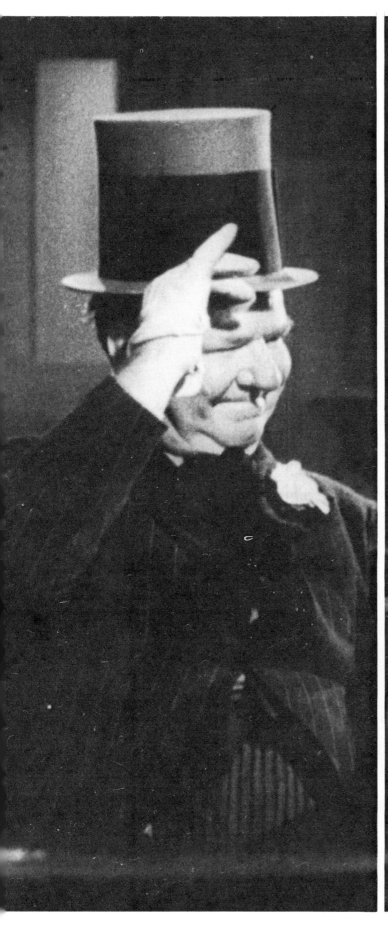

Twillie: May I present my card?

Mrs. Gideon: "Money loaned on jewelry, furs, clothing —"

Twillie: Just a moment. How did this get in there?

Mrs. Gideon: Thank you.

Mrs. Gideon: Was that chap dragging you across the prairie a full-blooded Indian?

Twillie: Full blooded? Quite the anthitheses. He's very anaemic.

Mrs. Gideon: Oh, what a pretty ring. Is it a cat's eye?

Twillie: Ah, yes, it is a cat's eye.

Mrs. Gideon: The pupil runs the wrong way. It's crossed.

Twillie: Crossed with a bob cat.

Twillie: Who's that vision of loveliness up there?

Twillie: Pardon me. I'll be back.
Mrs. Gideon: Go on.

Twillie: Pardon me.

Twillie: Nice day.

Flower: Is it?

Twillie: Of course, it's only one man's opinion.

Twillie: May I present my card?

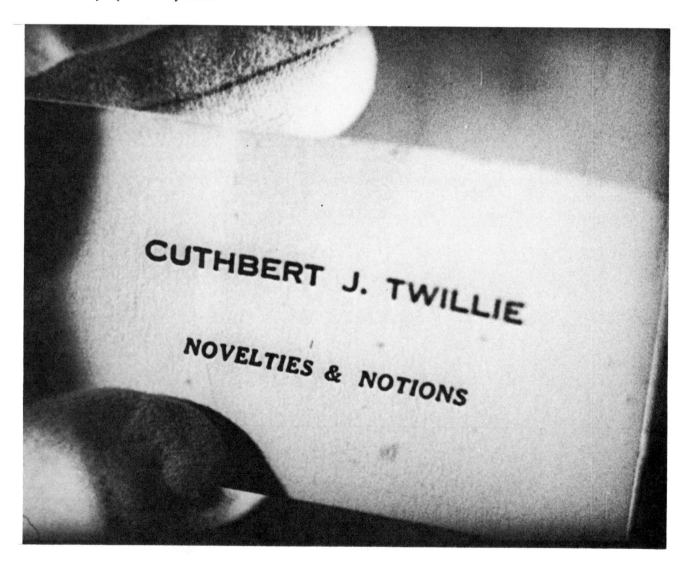

CUTHBERT J. TWILLIE

NOVELTIES & NOTIONS

Flower: "Novelties and notions." What kind of notions you got?

Twillie: You'd be surprised. Some are old and some are new.

Twillie: Whom have I the honor of addressing, Milady?

Flower: They call me Flower Belle.

Twillie: Flower Belle! What a euphonious appellation! Easy on the ears and a banquet for the eyes.

Flower: You're kinda cute yourself.

Twillie: Thank you. I never argue with a lady.   **Flower:** Smart boy.

LATER

Twillie: Tell me, my little prairie flower — can you give me the inside info on yon damsel with the hothouse cognomen?

Mrs. Gideon: You mean Miss Flower Belle Lee?

Twillie: I don't mean some woman out in China.

Mrs. Gideon: I'm afraid I can't say anything good about Flower.

Twillie: I can see what's good. Tell me the rest.

Mrs. Gideon: Because of her carryings on in Little Bend — she was asked to leave town. And she will not be permitted to return until she is respectable and married! And furthermore, I don't think she will be received in Greasewood City. In fact, I don't think she will be permitted to step off the train!

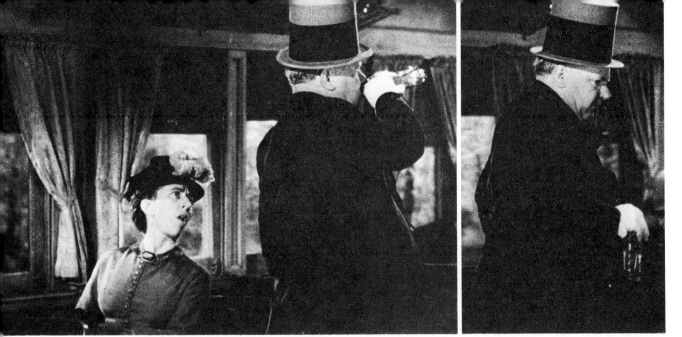

Mrs: Gideon: Oh! I hope that wasn't whiskey you were drinking!

Twillie: Oh no, my dear, just a little sheep dip. Panacea for all stomach ailments.

Twillie: Hmm! I hope she don't get too violent. I haven't strength enough to knock her down. Well, good-bye. The days of chivalry are not over.

Twillie: Baby doll — these weed benders have been running off at the mouth to your detriment.

Flower: I ain't surprised. Bad news travels fast.

Twillie: I understand you need a cicerone — a guide.

Flower: I need more than that, Honey.

Twillie: Ah! What symmetrical digits. Soft as the fuzz on a baby's arm.

Flower: But quick on the trigger.   **Twillie:** Yes — Yes. But, may I?

Flower: Help yourself.

Twillie: Would you object if I availed myself of the second helping.

Flower: Don't you think you're a little forward on such short acquaintance? You're compromising me.

Twillie: May I present you with a little amulet that I received from Aga Khan when I was in the Himalyas? It's just a little thing. The Aga and I were very good friends.

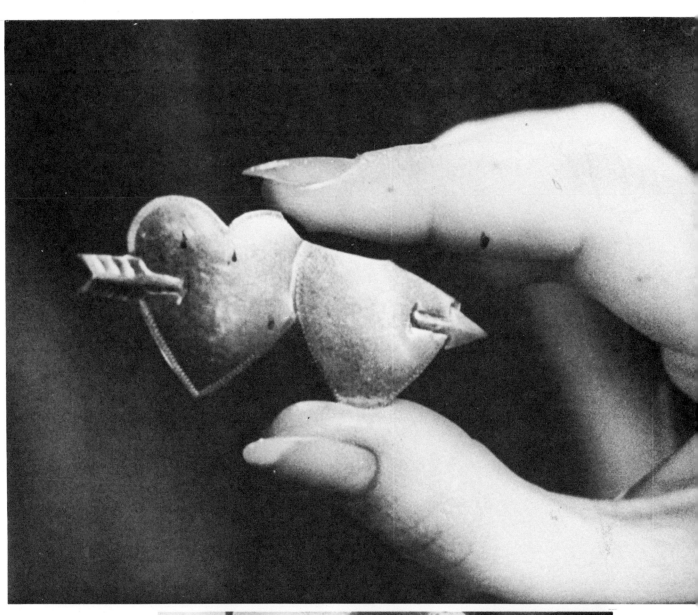

Flower: Oh! What a pretty sentiment.

Flower: It's no fun for a woman, either.

Twillie: A lonesome heart. That's what I am. It's not good for man to be alone.

Twillie: Is it possible for us to be lonesome together?

Flower: It is quite possible.

Twillie: I will be all things to you. Father, mother, husband, counsellor, Japanese bartender.

Flower: You're offering quite a bundle, Honey.

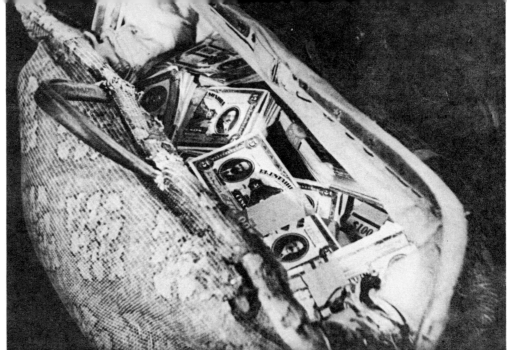

Twillie: My heart is a bargain today. Will you take me?

Flower: I'll take you — and how!

159

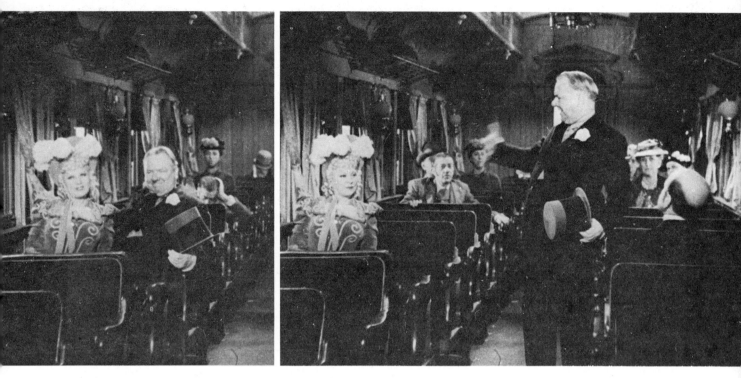

Twillie: I am the happiest mortal alive! Miss Flower Belle has consented to be my lawfully wedded wife!

Twillie: Now we'll need a ring.

Twillie: I think
I have one here
that will fit.

Twillie: The fourth digit of the left hand.

Twillie: Hmm. There! If I had a little goose grease. Perfect!

Flower Belle and Cuthbert Twillie arrive at their honeymoon hotel.

Twillie: This should make a cozy little nest.   **Flower:** Don't start crowing too soon.

Twillie: Crowing — very good — very good.   **Flower:** Two rooms — if you don't mind.

Twillie: Yes — the bridal suite. We're married, you know.

Flower: I'll take the suite. Give him the room.

Clerk: Yes, ma'am.

Twillie: But, my dove.

Twillie: My little dove! My little sugar-coated wedding cake.

Twillie: Come, my phlox, my flower. I have some very definite pear-shaped ideas I'd like to discuss with thee. Come — open.

Twillie: Egad! The child's afraid of me — she's all 'atwit.

Flower: You can't come in now. Go away. I'm dressing.

Twillie: I'm as gentle as a forest bred lion.

Flower: Get away from my keyhole.

Twillie: It was the cat, dear.

Flower: Oh, don't be old fashioned. Be a good boy and run along. Why don't you look the town over?

Twillie: Listen. Didn't you promise to love, honor and be obedient?

Twillie: What an unselfish little rose petal you are, to be sure.

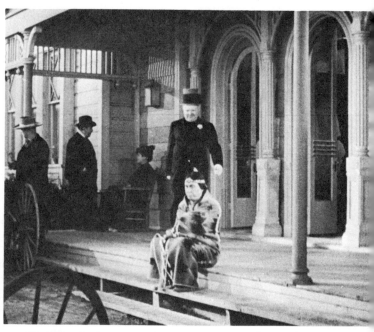

Twillie: Milton, my brave — go upstairs and pary your stoical presence outside the teepee of Mrs. Twillie. Number Eight.

Twillie: I'll proceed to the local gin mill and absorb a beaker of firewater.

Milton: Big Chief gottum new squaw?

Twillie: New is right. She hasn't been unwrapped yet.

No sense spending the evening alone!

Twillie: Playing a lone hand?

Man: Up to now.

Twillie: Would you like to engage in a little game of cut — high card wins?

Man: What stakes?

Twillie: Make it easy on yourslf.

Man: A hundred dollars, gold.

Twillie: I'll cover that. I'm traveling a little light. The country is fraught with marauders. I'll give you my personal I.O.U. A thing I seldom give to strangers.

Man: That I.O.U. better be good.

Twillie: Sweet and cold.

Man: King!

Twillie: Oh!

Twillie: Don't show it to me. The cards are a gentleman's game. I don't want to look at it.

Twillie: Ace!

179

Man: I didn't see it!

Twillie: Well, well, here you are —

Twillie: here you are, Nosy Parker — ace!

Twillie: I hope that satisfies your morbid curiosity.

Twillie: Shall we have another wager?

Twillie: Probably at some future day!

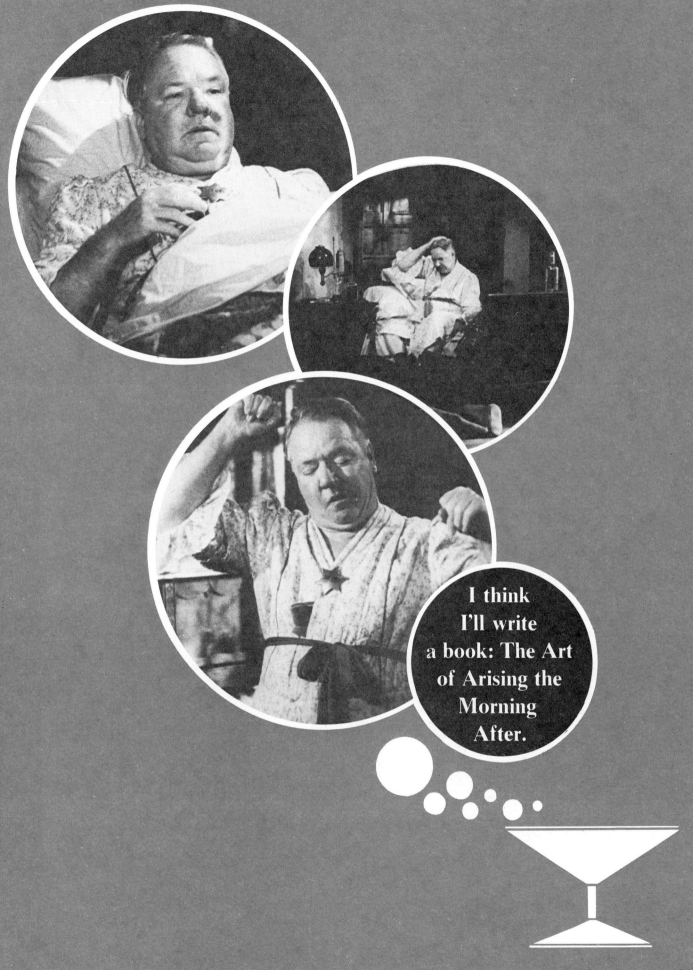

**There are
two sides to
every story.**

Twillie: I'm tendin' bar one time down in the lower East Side in New York — a tough paloma comes in there, by the name of Chicago Molly. I cautioned her: "None of your picadilloes in here."

There was some hot lunch on the bar, comprised of succatash, Philadelphia cream cheese and asparagus with mayonnaise.

She dips her mitt down into this moulage. I'm yawning at the time, and she hits me right in the mouth with it!

I jumps over the bar!
I knock her down! . . .

Squawk: Where's the funnel?

Twillie: I don't know — it's around somewhere.

Twillie: You were there the night I knocked Chicago Molly down, weren't you?

Squawk: *You* knocked her down! I was the one that knocked her down.

Twillie: Oh, yes-yes. You were the one that knocked her down, but I was the one that kicked her.

Twillie: Yes — okay . . . So I starts to kick her in the midriff. Did you ever kick a woman in the midriff that had a pair of corsets on?

Man: No. I just can't recall any such incident right now.

Twillie: Why. I almost broke my great toe. I never had such a painful experience.

Man: Did she ever come back again?

Squawk: I'll say she came back. She came back later and beat th' both of us up.

Twillie: Yes, but she had another woman with with her: an elderly lady with grey hair.

Have
you any
last wish?

Yes — I'd
like to see
Paris before
I die.

Uh, Philadelphia will do.

As proprietor of the Whipsnade Circus, Fields puts his grandfather's advice to good use.

Dave: There's a mistake in my change.

Whipsnade: Oh, at long last an honest man. You want to return some money?

Dave: No — I'm short.

Whipsnade: Don't brag about it. I'm only five feet eight myself.

Dave: Oh, I mean I'm short in my money.

Whipsnade: No mistakes rectified after once leaving the window.

Bill: You are dishonest!   **Whipsnade:** Me dishonest? Meishack, Shadrack and Abednego!

Dave: You cheated us.

Whipsnade: Sir, you impugn my honor, My dear old grandfather Litcock said, just before they sprung the trap, you can't cheat an honest man. Never give a sucker an even break or smarten up a chump.

Dave: We want what's coming to us!
Bill: And we're gonna get it, too!
Whipsnade: You are?
Dave: Yeh!
Whipsnade: You, too?
Dave: Yes. Come on — give it to us!
Whipsnade: You are both certainly going to get it.

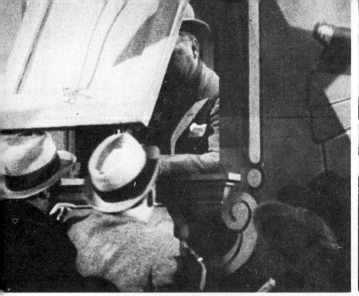

Attendant: What do you mean by creating a disturbance around the ticket window?

Dave: He cheated us, the big snozzle.

Whipsnade: In the snozzler — that's libelous.

Whipsnade: Demon rum! My heart bleeds for those poor boys.

**Fields and Charlie McCarthy go at
it in a fine example of their famous feud.**

Whipsnade: Right upon this platform . . . the world's greatest novelty — the Pronkwonk twins — Elwood and Brentwood — Elwood is ten minutes older than Brentwood and has been in a hurry ever since.

Whipsnade: Ladies and gentlemen — Brentwood is the smallest giant in the world — whilst his brother Elwood is the largest midget in the world.

Whipsnade: They baffle science.

Charlie: Say listen to that guy lie.

Whipsnade: Quiet — you termites' flophouse.

Charlie: Did you hear that . . . That's the last straw — I'm going.

Whipsnade: Now if you will take one short step with me to the —

Whipsnade: Ladies and gentlemen up — on this platform we have the Great Edgar and his whispering pine, Charlie McCarthy — they baffle science.

Charlie: Are you eating a tomato or is that your nose?

Bergen: Ssh!

 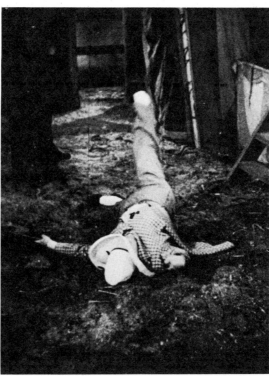 

Charlie: Upsie daisy — what a floparoo.

Whipsnade: Very good — very good Charles. You must come down with me after the show to the lumber yard and ride piggyback on the buzz saws.

Charlie: Nobody's going to find me after the show.

Whipsnade: Yes they are — you'll be hanging in my window as Venetian blinds.

Charlie: Oh, that makes me shudder.

Whipsnade: Quiet — or I'll throw a woodpecker on ya.

Cheerful: Boss.

Whipsnade: What?

Cheerful: It's time for your bath, suh.

Whipsnade: How time flies — it seems as though it was only Monday.

Cheerful: You sure runs on schedule.

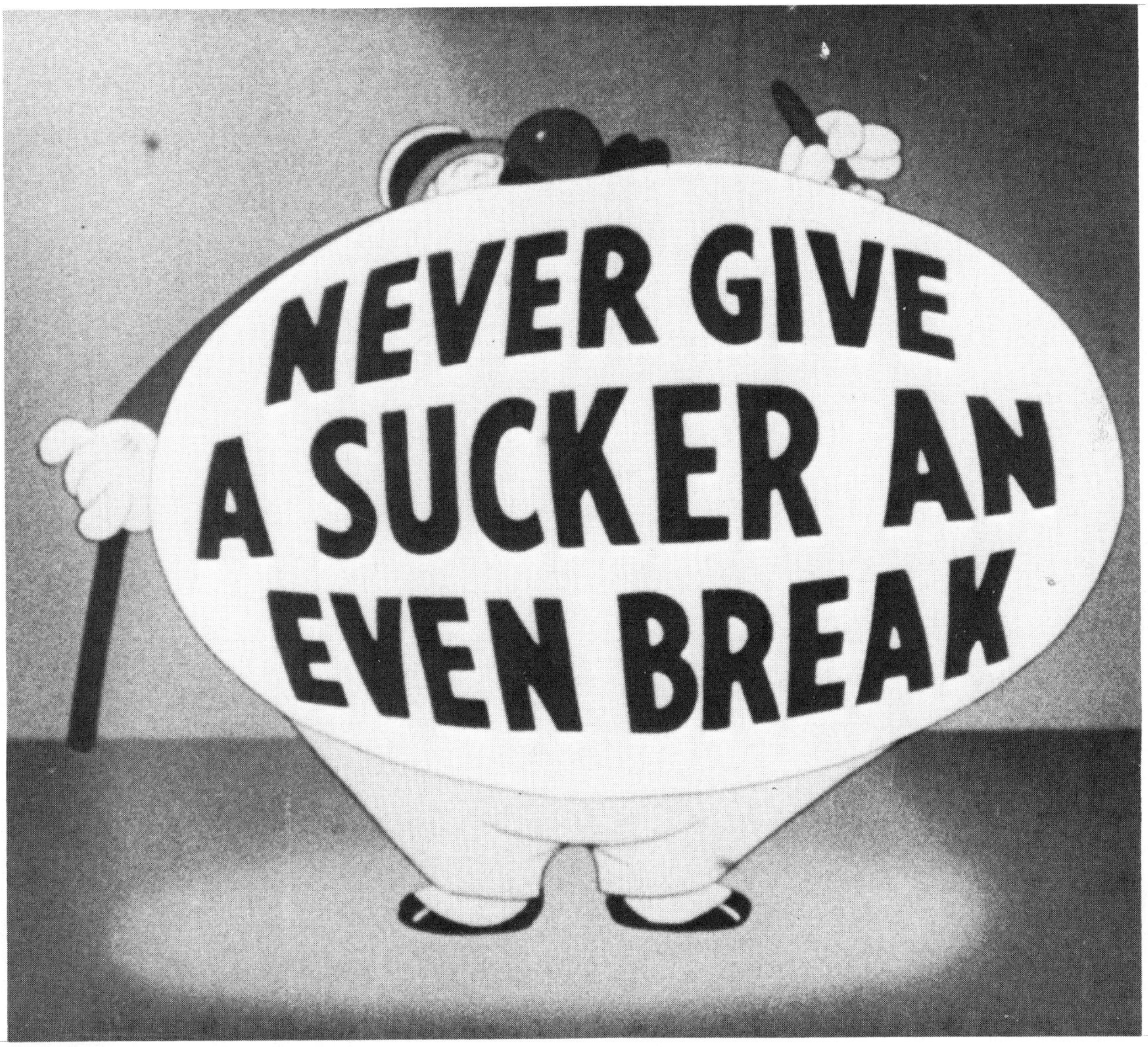
NEVER GIVE
A SUCKER AN
EVEN BREAK

**Fields decides
to compliment
a chickadee.**

Girl: Why — who are you talking to?

Fields: How are you Tootie-pie? Everything under control?

Fields: All five of them hit me at once.

Ordering breakfast could be an adventure in some establishments.

Fields: Ah, good morning Beautiful. What do you hear from Garcia?

Fields: Ah, ringer!

Fields: Got a menu?

Fields: Thank you. Thank you. Aaah!

Waitress: That's roast beef gravy.

Fields: Ah! Roast beef gravy.

Fields: Is that steak New York cut?

Fields: What about —

Fields:
No extra charge
for the cold shower,
I hope.

Fields: Do you think it's too hot for pork chops?

Fields: Ah! That practically eliminates everything but ham and eggs. Forgot about that. Er — no ham? Two fomented eggs in a glass.

Waitress: Cup.

Fields: Uh — yes — cup. And some whole wheat —

Waitress: White.

Fields: Yeah — some white bread. Yes.

Fields: And a cup of Mocha Java with cream.

Waitress: Milk.   **Fields:** Uh — milk. Yes. That's fine.

Waitress: Two in the water — easy!

214

Fields: I don't know why I ever come in here.
The flies get the best of everything.

Some short takes during a long flight.

Fields: What's the matter — did you sprain your ankle?

Englishman: Er — no — no — no — a dog — er — bit me.

Fields: Oh.

Englishman: I was playing, er croquet — and or I dropped my wallet and er —

Englishman: A little Daschund ran straight out and er — grabbed me by the fetlock.
Fields: Oh — rather fortunate that it wasn't a Newfoundland dog that bit you.

Stewardess: Time to get up, sir, we're landing shortly.

Fields: Ohhh!

Stewardess: Are you air sick?

Fields: No, dear, somebody put too many olives in my martini last night.

Stewardess: Could I get you a bromo?

Fields: No, I couldn't stand the noise.

You know,
Uncle Bill, I've been thinking. Why
didn't you ever marry?

I was in
love with a beautiful
blonde once, dear.
She drove me to drink.
That's the one thing
I'm indebted to
her for.

219

Gloria: We're falling two thousand feet!

Fields: It's all right, dear. Don't start worrying until we get down one thousand, nine hundred and ninety-nine. It's the last foot that's dangerous.

The unkindest cut of all.

Fields: Give me a drink. I'm dying.

Clerk: What'll it be?

Fields: Jumbo ice cream soda.

Clerk: What flavor?

Fields: Spinach, horse-radish — anything you've got there.

Clerk: I'll give you peach.

Fields: Whew! I feel as though somebody had stepped on my tongue with muddy feet.

Fields: This scene was supposed to be in a saloon, but the censor cut it out. It'll play just as well.

W.C. FIELDS

IN The Bank Dick

Original Screen Play

MAHATMA KANE JEEVES

Mother-in-law:
Smoking and drinking
and reading those infernal
detective stories. The house
just smells of liquor and
smoke.

**Egbert Sousé (Fields)
can't smoke or drink in his
own home; but he tries.**

Mother-in-law: There he goes again down to the saloon to read those silly detective magazines.

Agatha: Mother was right. You've been smoking again in your room.

Mother-in-law: Imagine a man who takes money out of a child's piggy bank and puts in I.O.U.'s.

Agatha: Don't you dare strike that child! You put that down! Put it down—put it down!

Myrtle: Og, I'd like you to meet my Father. Father — this is Og Oggilby.

Egbert: Og Oggilby.
Sounds like a bubble
in a bathtub.

Egbert: I'm glad
to have met you.

Og: I'm mighty
glad I met you.

Egbert: Are you carrying the proper amount of air in the tires? Had the brakes tested lately? Of course, it may

Egbert: What seems to be the trouble?

be the wheelbase.

Chauffeur: Why don't you go away and mind your own business?

Woman: Listen to the gentleman attentively, James. Be polite.

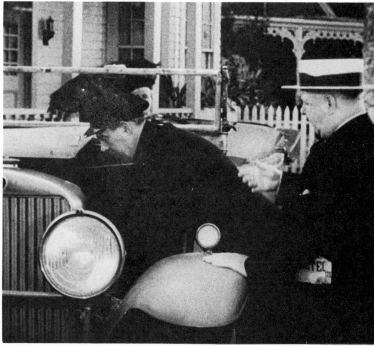

Egbert: Thank you, madam. Give me a shift expander — I'll fix it.

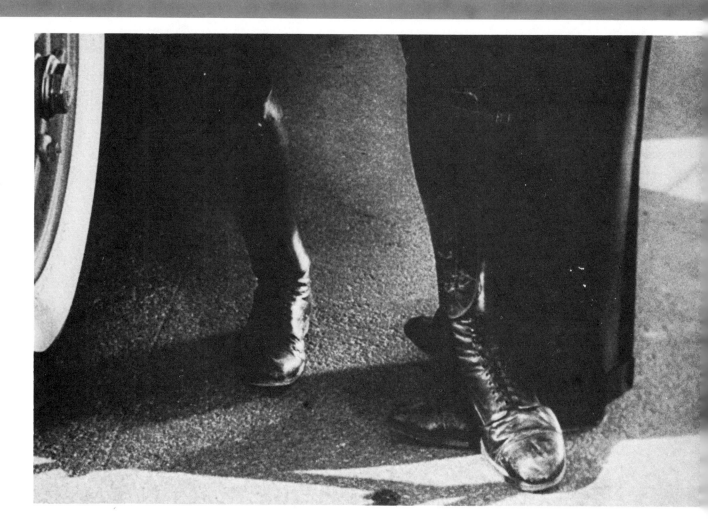

Chauffeur: A what?   **Egbert:** A monkey wrench.   **Woman:** Give the gentleman what he asks for, James.

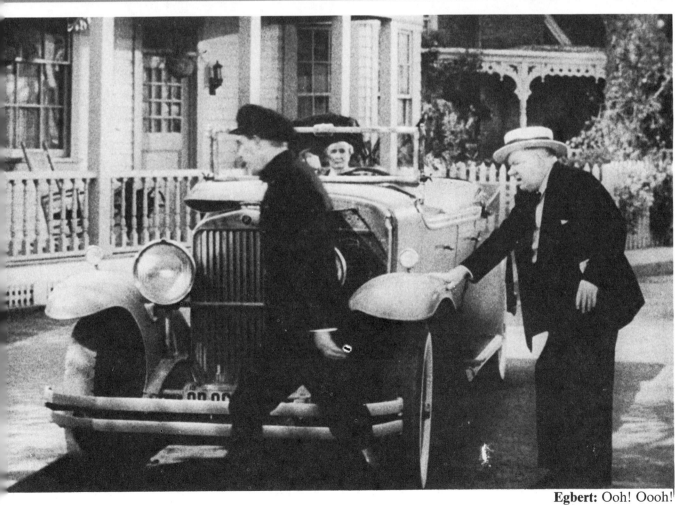

Egbert: Ooh! Oooh!

240

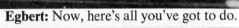
Egbert: Now, here's all you've got to do.

Egbert: Just open up this nut here.

The fine art of drinking...

Well — here she goes — down the hatch.

On the fine art of washing...

Was I in here last night and did I spend a twenty dollar bill?

Yeh!

Oh, boy! What a load that is off my mind! I thought I'd lost it.

Having proclaimed himself a veteran director, Sousé takes over the reins of a local production.

Egbert: That number seven expression. Who's on?

Elsie Mae: I want to be in a pitchur.

Egbert: I'll put you in later on, dear.

Elsie Mae: What's the matter, Pop, don't you love me?

Egbert: Love, I love —   **Agatha:** Don't you dare strike that child!

Egbert: She's not going to tell me I don't love her.

Francois:
Those eyes . . .
those eyes . . .
Those ears . . .
that nose.

Egbert:
Godfrey
Daniel!
Mother of
pearl!

Egbert: Murder!
Murder!

Agatha: The child is
only playing with
you — you fool!

Egbert: I don't
understand her funning.

Egbert: Well now,
to continue —

Egbert:
See you're
still at it.

Egbert:
Ow!

256

James: Serves you right.

Woman: Be courteous, James.

Hey, go on do another!

Oh boy — that's swell!

I'll teach you when you grow up. I never smoked a cigarette until I was nine.

**The bank dick
must be ever wary.**

Egbert: Get him — get him — here

Woman: What do you mean?

Egbert: Is that gun loaded?
Woman: Certainly not — but I think you are.

Boy: Mommie, doesn't that man have a funny nose?

Woman: You musn't make fun of the gentleman, Clifford. You'd like to have a nose like that full of nickels, wouldn't you?

Egbert: I'll throw him in the waste paper basket next time he comes in here.

Having redirected some of the bank's assets, Sousé tries to stall the bank examiner (Franklin Pangborn).

Egbert: The Black Pussy Cafe and snack bar. How would you like to go in and have a little spot?

Snoop: No thank you. I never drink during business hours.

Egbert: Just a little spot and we'll find out how Gumlegs made out at Del Mar today.

Snoop: This place isn't crowded, is it?

Egbert: No, if it wasn't for me, this place would starve to death.

Snoop: I'll just daudle about ten minutes.

Egbert: We'll both daudle together.

Snoop: Could we find a secluded spot where we won't be observed?

Egbert: Oh, sure. Sit right down and nobody will see you. These people are all right. Just a couple of local beer gouzzlers.

Snoop: Can't we, eh, pull the shade.

Egbert: You can pull anything you want in here. It's a regular joint. I know him very well. What's your pleasure?

Snoop: A rye highball . . .
Light.

Egbert: Right.

Egbert: Eh, hello, Joe.

Joe: Hello, Mr. Souse.
What'll you have?

Egbert: I want two highballs
One very light — you can
double up on mine.

Egbert: Has Michael Finn been
in here today?

Joe: No, but he will be.

Egbert: How did Gumlegs come out in the fifth?

Joe: He ran sixth.

Egbert: Oh.

Egbert: The dog, ever bet on the races?

Snoop: No, I never wager.

Egbert: You never wager. It's not a bad idea. It's a good system.

Egbert: I bet on that Gumlegs once. He won.

The jockey got off at the three quarter and had to carry him across the tape on his back. He's a beetle.

Egbert: The jockey was a very insulting fella — he referred to my proboscis as an adsatious exrescious. I was compelled to . . .

Well, down the hatch.

Even in Fields' day, the phone company could be relied upon for prompt and courteous service.

Operator: When you hear the tone—it will be twenty two and one half minutes til seven.

Egbert: Listen — I'm calling Doctor Stall and as a matter of fact it will be twenty two and one half minutes til six. Gimme Dr. Stall.

Operator: I'll give you information please.

Egbert: I don't want information please — or professor quiz or calling all cars — I want Dr. Stall.

Operator: Louder please.

Egbert: Louder please — if I spoke any louder I wouldn't need a telephone. Gimme Dr. Stall.